ANSWERS

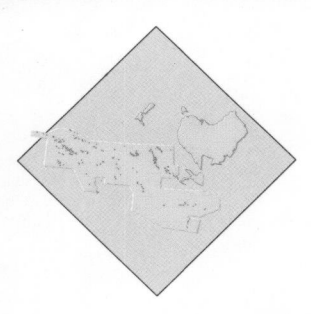

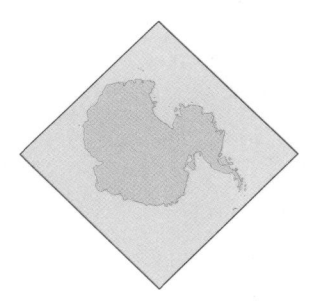

36 In which country are the Cambrian Mountains?

37 In which year did Mt. Vesuvius erupt destroying the city of Pompeii?

38 If you were skiing in the High Tatras, which country would you be in?

39 Where is the Wailing Wall?

40 What is the main product of Brunei?

41 How many active volcanoes are there in Japan?

42 In which country is the Serengeti Wildlife Park?

43 What ancient civilisation was based in the Yucatan in Mexico?

44 Gauchos are found in which country?

45 Where in the world would you find a Macaroni and an Emperor?

46 What countries were the six founder members of the European Union?

47 Name the capital of the Central African Republic?

48 What currency is used in the USA?

49 What is the longest river in Europe?

50 Name the sea between Australia and New Zealand?

Quiz continues at back.

Answers for questions 1-50 at back.

COLLINS

Children's Atlas

OF THE WORLD

HarperCollins*Publishers*

Published by Bartholomew
a division of HarperCollins Publishers
77-85 Fulham Palace Road
London W6 8JB

First published in 1991
New edition 1994
© Copyright Bartholomew 1991, 1994

The contents of this edition of the Children's Atlas of the World are
believed to be correct at the time of printing. Nevertheless, the publishers
can accept no responsibility for errors, or for omissions, or for changes in
detail given.

Printed in Hong Kong
ISBN 0 00 448131 3

Photograph Credits

J. Allan Cash Photo Library
Robert Harding Picture Library
Zefa Picture Library (UK) Ltd
Susan Griggs Agency
Hutchison Library
Forestry Commission
British Antarctic Survey/M Thomson
Russia and Republics Photo Library
Tom Van Sant/Science Photo Library
B and C Alexander
1992 Comstok/Nik Wheel/SGC
Telegraph Colour Library

COLLINS
Children's Atlas
OF THE WORLD

Globes and maps

It was not until the 1960's that it was possible to take photographs of the Earth from space. The first people to see the Earth from space were the astronauts on Apollo 8 in 1968.

The globes in these photographs of the earth were made up from thousands of cloud-free satellite images. The photographs show the Earth as it would appear if there were no clouds. Each photograph shows a different view of the Earth. Looking down the page from the top the photographs show the Earth as it revolves in space from west to east. The oceans and continents can easily be seen. The oceans cover more than two-thirds of the surface of the earth. The land, or continents, cover the rest.

The Atlantic Ocean, Europe, Africa and part of Asia can be seen on this photograph. The land at the left-hand edge is South America. ▶

This photograph also shows the Atlantic Ocean and, in the centre, North America and South America. Part of the Pacific Ocean is on ◀ the left of the photograph.

Australasia is at the centre of this photograph with parts of Asia to the north. The ice covered continent at the bottom of the photograph is Antarctica. ▼

The whole of Asia can be seen in this ▶ *photograph, with part of Europe and Africa also appearing to the west. The Indian Ocean is in the bottom centre of the photograph.*

A globe, like the one shown in the photographs on these pages, is the only way to show the shape of the Earth accurately. A globe also shows the oceans and the continents in the correct position and how large they are compared to each other.

A drawing or map made from one view of the Earth will only show some of the continents and oceans. The only way to show the whole of the Earth's curved surface accurately would be to split it into different parts or segments. To be able to show the whole of the earth's surface on a map in one piece, the continents and oceans have to be stretched or shrunk. It is possible to recognise the oceans and continents but both their shape and size compared to each other has been changed on the maps.

This photograph of the globe shows most of North America, Europe and part of Asia and Africa. The white mass in the top centre is the ice in the Arctic Ocean at the North Pole.

This map shows the same part of the Earth as the photograph above. It shows land and sea.

This map shows the whole of the earth's surface. The shapes and sizes of the oceans and continents have had to be stretched or shrunk.

▲ *This map shows the whole of the earth's surface, but it is split into different parts or segments. It is difficult to put names on a map like this.*

World maps also make the Earth look as if it has edges. It is important to remember that, on the map on the right, the ocean on the left is part of the ocean on the right and Antarctica, spread out along the bottom of the map, is one continent.

5

Satellite images and maps

This satellite image, or photograph, shows the northern part of the United Kingdom. The shape of the land can be seen against the dark blue of the sea. The many islands to the west and north of Scotland stand out clearly.

The hills and mountains looks like thin pieces of creased paper and the lakes are dark blue like the sea. The different colours on the photograph show the grassland, moorland, forests and farmland with crops.

The photograph shows the shape of the land and where different features like islands and lakes are in comparison to each other. The photograph does not show the names of the islands and lakes. The photograph is too small to show where towns and cities are.

SATELLITE IMAGE

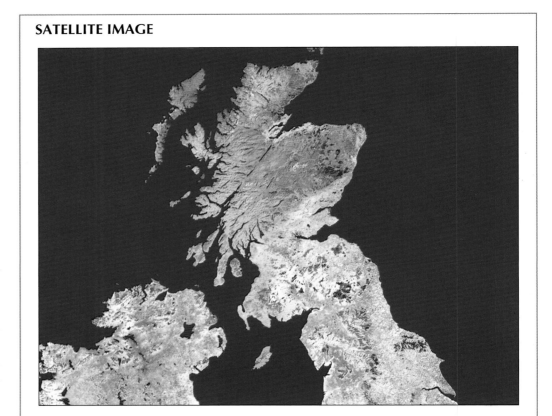

The map shows the same part of the United Kingdom. The map shows different information from the photograph. Names have been added to the map to show where places are. This map shows country names, city and town names and the names of mountains and islands. The position of cities and towns is shown by a red and black dot.

The colours on this map show the height of the land. Other maps in the atlas show different information by using colour to show where countries are or where a special feature is. The map on page 30 uses a special colour to show the area of the Roman Empire.

MAP

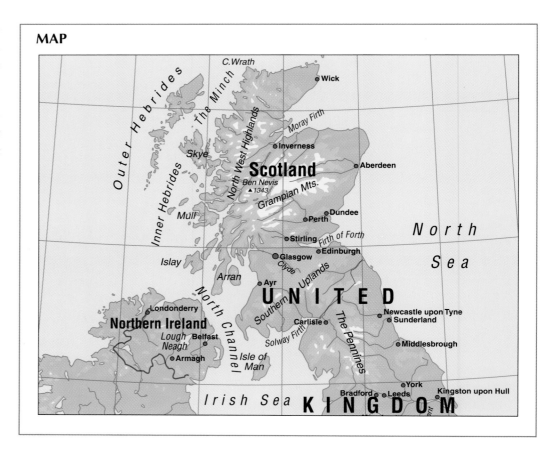

Scale

Anything drawn on a map is smaller on the map than it is in real life. The map scale shows how much smaller than real life things have been drawn on the map. The scale on the maps in this atlas are shown two different ways:

a line or linear scale and a representative fraction scale:

1 : 5 000 000

Each section on the linear scale shows the distance on the map equal to 50 kilometres on the ground. The distance between two places can be measured using the linear scale.

The representative fraction scale means that 1 centimetre on the map is equal to 5 000 000 centimetres or 50 kilometres on the ground. The representative fraction scale allows the scale of two different maps to be compared.

The map of Southwest England on this page is at a scale of 1: 5 000 000 and the map of Europe is at a scale of 1:100 000 000. This means that the scale of the map of England is twenty times larger than the scale of the map of Europe.

The scale of a map also affects the amount of information and the area of land that can be shown on the map. The map of Southwest England at 1:5 000 000 shows towns and cities, but the map at 1:20 000 000 can only show the shape of the whole of the British Isles.

The three maps opposite each cover the same space on the page, but as the scale becomes smaller a much larger area of land can be shown in the same space.

SOUTHWEST ENGLAND

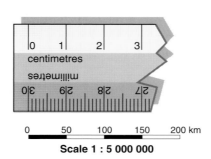

Scale 1 : 5 000 000

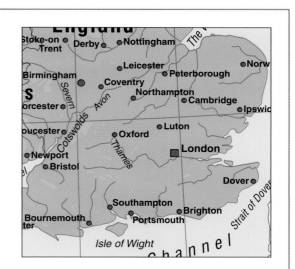

This map shows the location of cities and towns and landscape features.

BRITISH ISLES

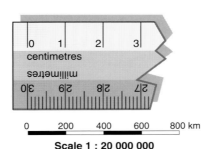

Scale 1 : 20 000 000

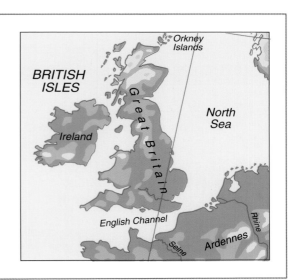

At this scale there is less detail, but a larger area of land is shown.

EUROPE

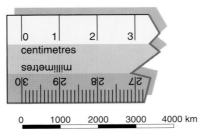

Scale 1 : 100 000 000

On this map, much less detail can be shown, but the whole of Europe and part of Africa is shown.

Location, map keys and symbols

This atlas is split into different sections. The first part of the atlas gives information about the continents, countries, climates and natural regions of the world. The rest of the atlas is split into continent sections. Each showing the landscapes and a map showing the countries of each continent. Following this there are maps of the countries and regions in that continent. As well as maps there are photographs, flags and fact files on each country. This page explains where to find the information on these country and region maps.

The location box shows the position of the country or region in the continent. Each continent has been given a different colour.

The flag box shows the national flag of each independent country on the map.

The fact file gives information about the capital city, area, population, language and money for the countries on the map.

The key box explains the colours and symbols used on the maps. More information about symbols is given on page 9.

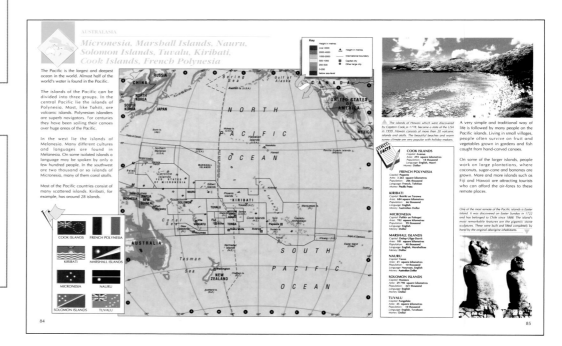

FINDING PLACES

At the beginning of the atlas there is a list of page titles and page numbers. To find a continent, region or country look at this list and find the page number.

To find a city, town or landscape feature such as an island or river, look at the Index on page 92 to 95 of the atlas. This list of names is arranged in alphabetical order. Each entry is organised in a particular way.

Honolulu 85 D5

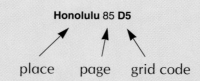

place   page   grid code

The entry starts with the place name, then the page number on which the map appears, then the grid code.

The grid code starts with a letter, these letters are along the top and bottom of the map. After the letter there is a number. The numbers are at the sides of the map. To find a place, find the grid letter and the grid number, look up or down the letter column to find where the columns meet, this is the grid square where the place is located. Search the grid square to find the place name.

There are different types of maps in this atlas, each type of map showing different information. Some maps show the shape of the land, others where landscape features, cities and towns are located.

A map selects and simplifies information by using symbols. Symbols can be the colours used to show different countries, or the colours used to show the height of the land. The shapes used to show cities and towns and the lines used to show rivers and boundaries are also symbols.

The different types of symbols used on each map in the atlas are explained in the key to each map.

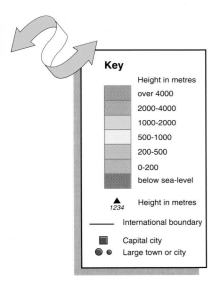

The names on the maps are shown in different styles of lettering. Each group of features such as country names or town names are all shown in the same style of lettering. This makes it easier to identify features and understand the map. The different styles of lettering are explained on the maps on this page. The same style of lettering is used on all the maps in the atlas.

CONTINENT MAPS *Countries*

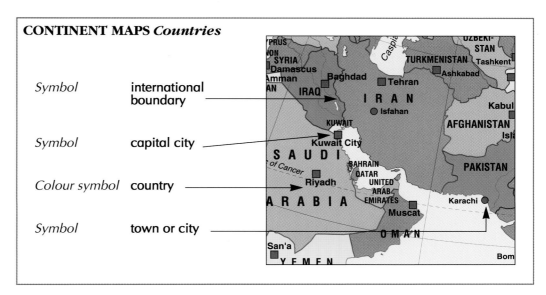

Symbol	international boundary
Symbol	capital city
Colour symbol	country
Symbol	town or city

CONTINENT MAPS *Landscape*

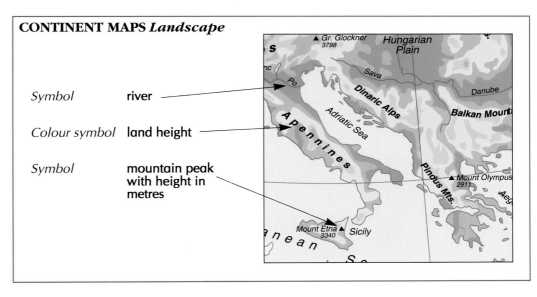

Symbol	river
Colour symbol	land height
Symbol	mountain peak with height in metres

Region and country maps

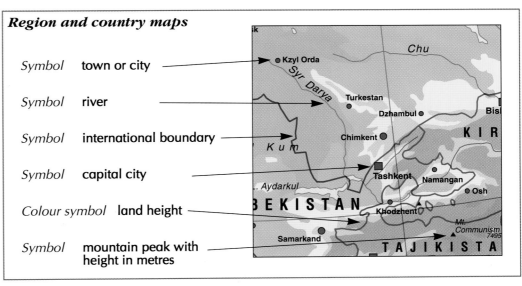

Symbol	town or city
Symbol	river
Symbol	international boundary
Symbol	capital city
Colour symbol	land height
Symbol	mountain peak with height in metres

9

The Continents

The land areas on the Earth's surface are divided into seven continents. Europe, Asia and Africa are joined together to make the largest land mass. North and South America are also linked and stretch most of the way from the North Pole to the South Pole. The other two continents, Australasia and Antarctica, stand on their own, separated from the rest.

There are high mountains and long rivers in most of the continents. Most of the world's highest mountains are in the Himalaya, in Asia. There are no rivers in Antarctica because it is too cold.

The largest lake is the Caspian Sea which is bigger than the whole of the British Isles. The largest Island in the world, Australia, is so big it is often called a continent.

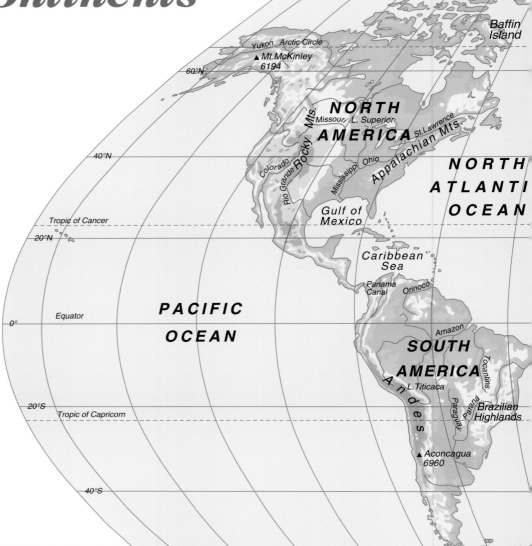

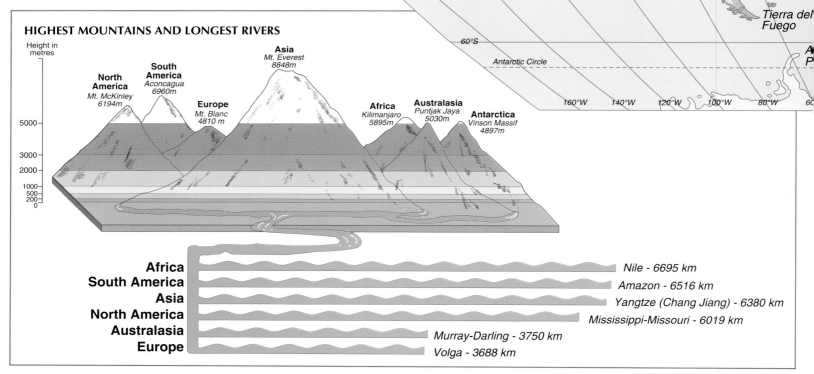

HIGHEST MOUNTAINS AND LONGEST RIVERS

Height in metres

Asia
Mt. Everest
8848m

North America
Mt. McKinley
6194m

South America
Aconcagua
6960m

Europe
Mt. Blanc
4810 m

Africa
Kilimanjaro
5895m

Australasia
Puntjak Jaya
5030m

Antarctica
Vinson Massif
4897m

Africa — Nile - 6695 km
South America — Amazon - 6516 km
Asia — Yangtze (Chang Jiang) - 6380 km
North America — Mississippi-Missouri - 6019 km
Australasia — Murray-Darling - 3750 km
Europe — Volga - 3688 km

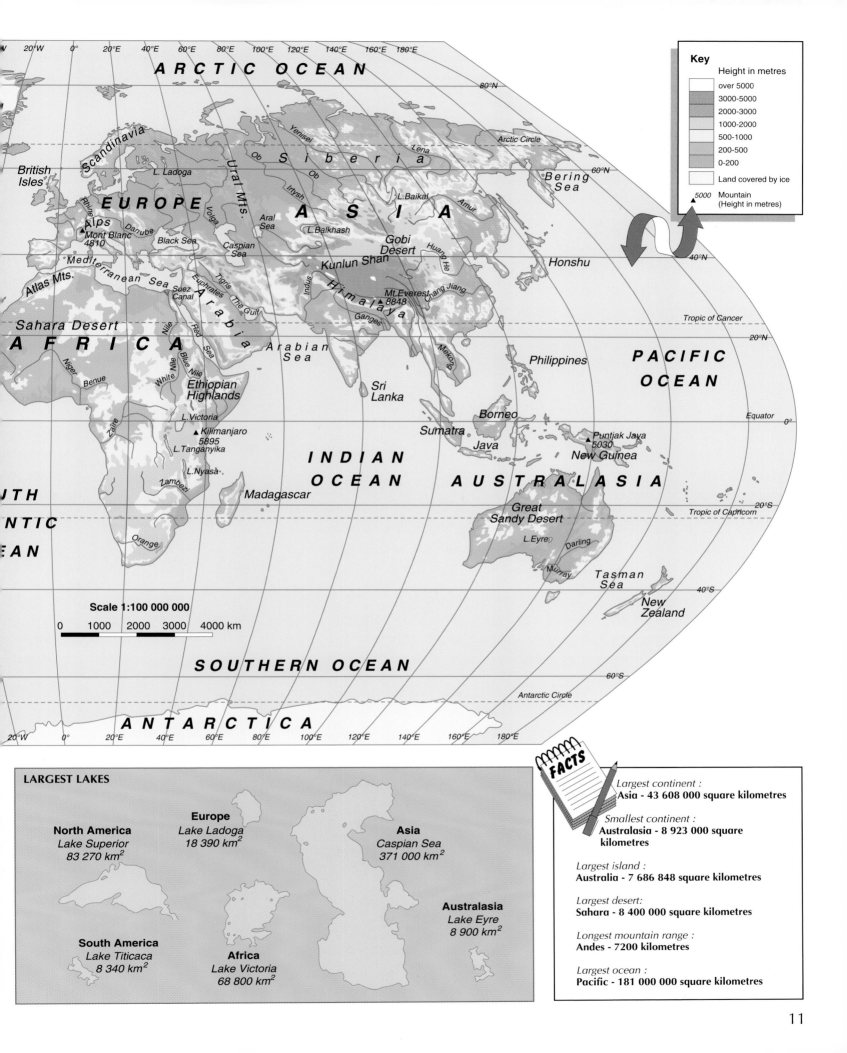

ARCTIC OCEAN

EUROPE · ASIA · AFRICA · AUSTRALASIA · ANTARCTICA

PACIFIC OCEAN · INDIAN OCEAN · SOUTHERN OCEAN

Key

Height in metres

- over 5000
- 3000-5000
- 2000-3000
- 1000-2000
- 500-1000
- 200-500
- 0-200
- Land covered by ice

▲5000 Mountain (Height in metres)

Scale 1:100 000 000

0 1000 2000 3000 4000 km

LARGEST LAKES

North America
Lake Superior
83 270 km²

Europe
Lake Ladoga
18 390 km²

Asia
Caspian Sea
371 000 km²

Australasia
Lake Eyre
8 900 km²

South America
Lake Titicaca
8 340 km²

Africa
Lake Victoria
68 800 km²

FACTS

Largest continent :
Asia - 43 608 000 square kilometres

Smallest continent :
Australasia - 8 923 000 square kilometres

Largest island :
Australia - 7 686 848 square kilometres

Largest desert:
Sahara - 8 400 000 square kilometres

Longest mountain range :
Andes - 7200 kilometres

Largest ocean :
Pacific - 181 000 000 square kilometres

Countries

ARCTIC OCEAN

GREENLAND

Arctic Circle

ICELAND

U.S.A. (Alaska)

■ Godthåb

■ Reykjavik

Oslo

C A N A D A

UNITED KINGDOM

DENMA

Dublin

IRELAND

London

1

GERM

■ Ottawa

Paris

2 3

FRANCE

4

UNITED STATES OF AMERICA

PORTUGAL

■ Madrid

Rom

Lisbon

SPAIN

■ Washington

N O R T H

Rabat

MOROCCO

Algiers

TU
Tr

A T L A N T I C

ALGERIA

O C E A N

Tropic of Cancer

BAHAMAS

MAURITANIA

MALI

NIGE

MEXICO

Havana

■ Nouakchott

CUBA

DOMINICAN REPUBLIC

Dakar

SENEGAL

Bamako

■ Niamey

Mexico City

20

HAITI

PUERTO RICO

21

GUINEA

BURKINA

23

N'Dji

BELIZE

JAMAICA

Conakry

Ab

GUATEMALA

Freetown

IVORY COAST

GHANA

22

NIGERIA

HONDURAS

SIERRA LEONE

EL SALVADOR

NICARAGUA

Monrovia

Accra

CAM

COSTA RICA

PANAMA

TRINIDAD AND TOBAGO

LIBERIA

Yaoundé

Caracas

EQUATORIAL GUINEA

VENEZUELA

GUYANA

SURINAM

FRENCH GUIANA

Libreville

GA

■ Bogotá

COLOMBIA

Braz

Equator

ANGOL

Quito

ECUADOR

Lua

P A C I F I C

PERU

B R A Z I L

O C E A N

■ Lima

■ La Paz

■ Brasilia

S O U T H

BOLIVIA

A T L A N T I C

PARAGUAY

O C E A N

Tropic of Capricorn

W

Asunción

CHILE

ARGENTINA

URUGUAY

Santiago

■ Montevideo

Ca

Buenos Aires

Key

■ Capital City

Numbered Countries

1	NETHERLANDS
2	BELGIUM
3	LUXEMBOURG
4	SWITZERLAND
5	AUSTRIA
6	CZECH REPUBLIC
7	SLOVAKIA
8	HUNGARY
9	SLOVENIA
10	CROATIA
11	BOSNIA-HERZEGOVINA
12	YUGOSLAVIA
13	ALBANIA
14	MACEDONIA
15	MOLDAVIA
16	ARMENIA
17	AZERBAIJAN
18	UNITED ARAB EMIRATES
19	BANGLADESH
20	GAMBIA
21	GUINEA BISSAU
22	TOGO
23	BENIN

Falkland Islands (U.K)

ARCTIC OCEAN

Arctic Circle

R U S S I A

Moscow

Kiev
RAINE
USSIA

KAZAKHSTAN

Ulan Bator

MONGOLIA

GEORGIA
TURKMENISTAN
UZBEKISTAN
16 17 Baku
Ankara
TURKEY

Alma-Ata
Bishkek
KIRGHIZIA
TAJIKISTAN
Ashkhabad Dushanbe

Beijing

NORTH
KOREA
Pyongyang
Seoul
SOUTH
KOREA

JAPAN

Tokyo

CHINA

SYRIA
Damascus
LEBANON
IRAQ
ISRAEL Baghdad
Cairo JORDAN
IRAN
Tehran
Kabul
AFGHANISTAN
Islamabad

KUWAIT
EGYPT
Riyadh QATAR
SAUDI 18
ARABIA
hartoum
SUDAN

PAKISTAN
New Delhi
NEPAL
BHUTAN

19
Dhaka

BURMA
(MYANMA)

LAOS
Hanoi

HONG
KONG

Taibei

TAIWAN

Tropic of Cancer

P A C I F I C

O C E A N

Muscat

OMAN

INDIA

ERITREA San'a
Asmara YEMEN
DJIBOUTI
Addis Ababa
ETHIOPIA
SOMALIA
Mogadishu

Vientiane
Yangon
(Rangoon)
THAILAND
Bangkok

VIETNAM

CAMBODIA
Rhnom
Penh

Manila

PHILIPPINES

SRI
LANKA
Colombo

UGANDA
Kampala KENYA
RWANDA Nairobi
BURUNDI
TANZANIA
Dodoma

BRUNEI
Kuala Lumpur MALAYSIA
SINGAPORE

INDIAN

OCEAN

I N D O N E S I A

PAPUA
NEW GUINEA

SOLOMON
ISLANDS

Equator

AMBIA
a
arare
IMBABWE
MOZAMBIQUE

MALAWI

MADAGASCAR
Antananarivo
MAURITIUS

Jakarta

Port
Moresby

A U S T R A L I A

Tropic of Capricorn

Maputo
SWAZILAND
oria
LESOTHO

Canberra

Scale 1 : 62 000 000

Wellington

NEW
ZEALAND

S O U T H E R N   O C E A N

Climate and Natural Regions

Rainfall and temperature are the main elements that go to make up climate. Generally, the places around the equator are hottest and those around the North and the South Poles are coldest. Rain does not fall evenly around the world, but depends on the direction of the wind and the height of the land. The types of trees and plants that grow depend on the climate.

The climate has a major effect on the natural environment. Five broad categories of natural region can be identified. However within these regions there are many variations due to the influences of the climate.

FACTS

Hottest place :
58°C Al'Aziziyah, Libya 1922

Coldest place :
-89°C Vostok, Antarctica 1988

Wettest place :
11 770mm average annual rainfall Tutunendo, Colombia

Driest place :
Calama, Atacama Desert, Chile - no rain for several hundred years

POLAR ZONE

Polar climates are cold throughout the year. Moisture falls as snow and there are many storms and blizzards. Few plants can grow in these conditions.

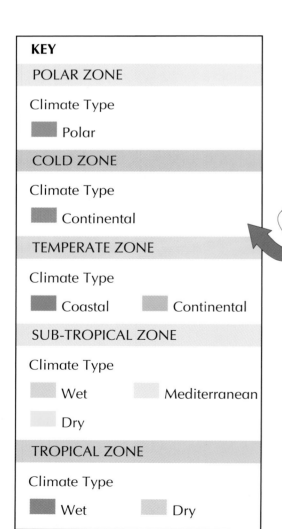

KEY

POLAR ZONE

Climate Type

☐ Polar

COLD ZONE

Climate Type

☐ Continental

TEMPERATE ZONE

Climate Type

☐ Coastal ☐ Continental

SUB-TROPICAL ZONE

Climate Type

☐ Wet ☐ Mediterranean

☐ Dry

TROPICAL ZONE

Climate Type

☐ Wet ☐ Dry

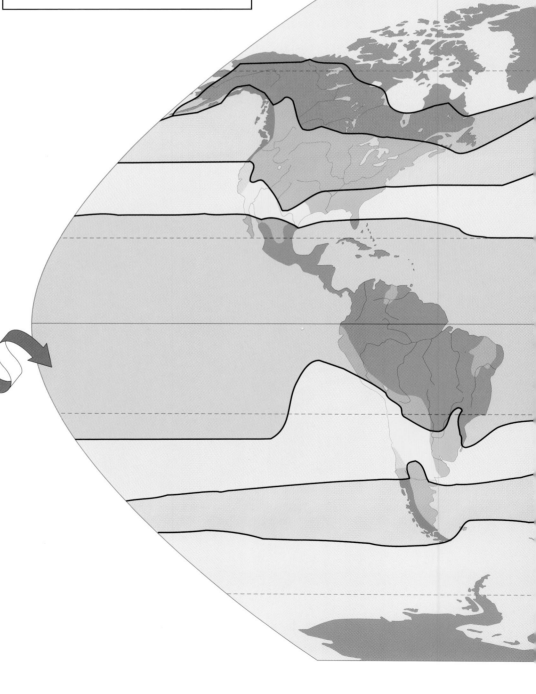

COLD ZONE

This zone has great extremes in temperature. Winters are very cold but summers are hot. There is rain or snow all year. Most of this zone is covered by coniferous forests.

TEMPERATE ZONE

The western coastal areas are mild and wet. The areas inland and on the east coasts are colder in winter but warmer in summer. Many different types of trees and plants grow.

SUB - TROPICAL ZONE

All climate types have hot summers and mild winters but different amounts of rainfall. Wet areas have over 1000mm of rain in a year while some dry areas have less than 250mm and are deserts.

TROPICAL ZONE

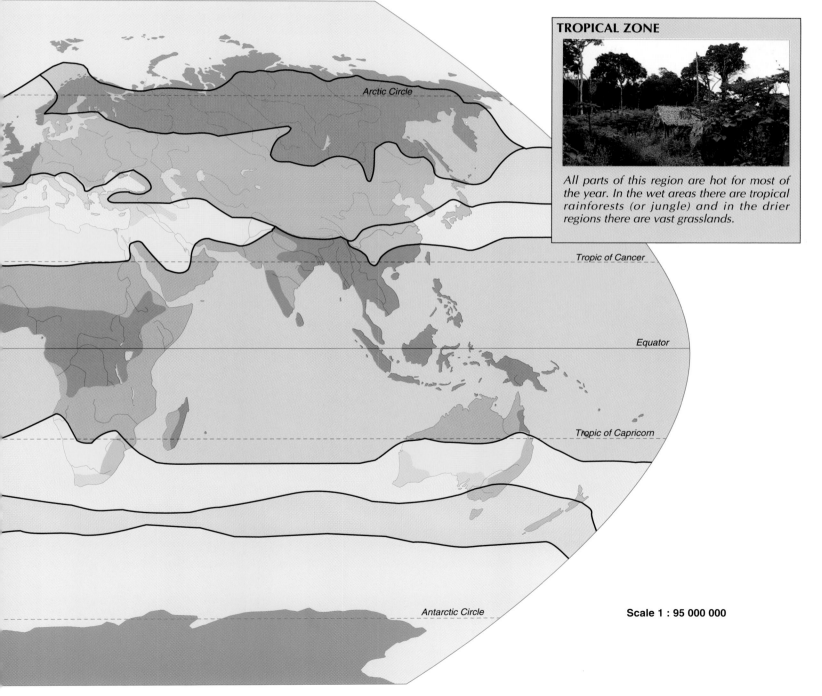

All parts of this region are hot for most of the year. In the wet areas there are tropical rainforests (or jungle) and in the drier regions there are vast grasslands.

Arctic Circle

Tropic of Cancer

Equator

Tropic of Capricorn

Antarctic Circle

Scale 1 : 95 000 000

Countries

Key

— International boundary

■ Capital city

● Other large city

ARCTIC OCEAN

ICELAND
Reykjavik

ATLANTIC OCEAN

NORWAY
SWEDEN
FINLAND
Helsinki
St Petersburg
Oslo
Stockholm
Tallinn
ESTONIA

RUSSIA
Moscow

North Sea

Edinburgh
Belfast
UNITED KINGDOM
REPUBLIC OF IRELAND
Dublin

DENMARK
Copenhagen

Riga
LATVIA
LITHUANIA
Vilnius
Minsk
BELORUSSIA

Hamburg
NETHERLANDS
Amsterdam
London
Rotterdam
Brussels
BELGIUM
LUXEMBOURG
Bonn
GERMANY
Berlin
POLAND
Warsaw
RUSSIA
Kiev
UKRAINE

Paris
Prague
CZECH REPUBLIC
SLOVAKIA
Bratislava

FRANCE
Munich
Vienna
AUSTRIA
Budapest
MOLDAVIA
Kishinev
Odessa
Sea of Azov

SWITZERLAND
Berne
SLOVENIA
HUNGARY
ROMANIA

Bordeaux
Lyon
Turin
Milan
Ljubljana
Zagreb
CROATIA
Belgrade
Bucharest
Black Sea

Vigo
ANDORRA
BOSNIA-HERZEGOVINA
Sarajevo
YUGOSLAVIA
BULGARIA
Sofia

SPAIN
Lisbon
PORTUGAL
Madrid
Barcelona
Corsica
ITALY
Rome
ALBANIA
Tiranë
Skopje
MACEDONIA
Istanbul
TURKEY

Valencia
Gibraltar (U.K)
Balearic Islands
Naples
Sardinia
GREECE
ASIA

Mediterranean Sea
Palermo
Sicily
Athens
Rhodes

AFRICA
MALTA
Crete

Scale 1 : 20 000 000
0 200 400 600 800 km

Arctic Circle

16

Landscape

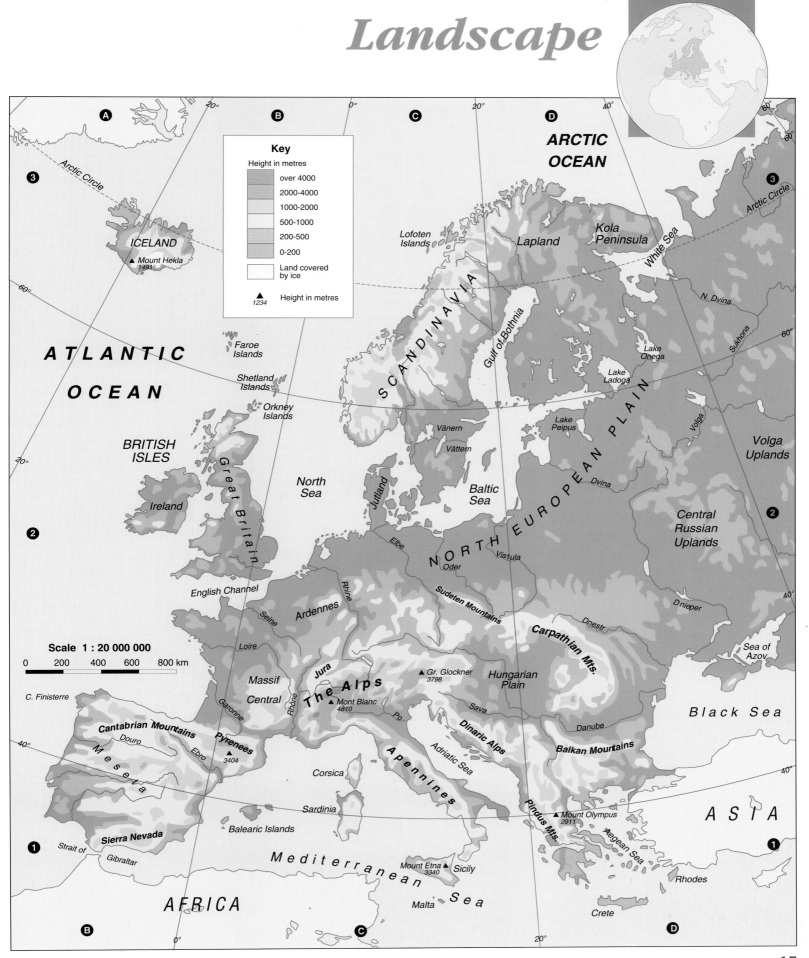

Key

Height in metres

- over 4000
- 2000-4000
- 1000-2000
- 500-1000
- 200-500
- 0-200
- Land covered by ice

▲ 1234 Height in metres

A **B** 0° **C** 20° **D** 40°

ARCTIC OCEAN

Arctic Circle

3 ICELAND ▲ Mount Hekla 1491

ATLANTIC OCEAN

Faroe Islands

Shetland Islands

Orkney Islands

BRITISH ISLES

Ireland Great Britain

North Sea

2

English Channel

Seine

Loire

Ardennes

Rhine

Massif Central

Jura

The Alps ▲ Gr. Glockner 3798

▲ Mont Blanc 4810

Rhône

Garonne

Cantabrian Mountains Pyrenees ▲ 3404

Douro

Ebro

M e s e t a

Sierra Nevada

Strait of Gibraltar

C. Finisterre

Scale 1 : 20 000 000

0 200 400 600 800 km

Corsica

Sardinia

Balearic Islands

M e d i t e r r a n e a n   S e a

Mount Etna 3340 ▲ Sicily

Malta

AFRICA

Lofoten Islands

Lapland

Kola Peninsula

White Sea

S C A N D I N A V I A

Gulf of Bothnia

Vänern

Vättern

Baltic Sea

Lake Onega

Lake Ladoga

Lake Peipus

N. Dvina

Sukhona

Volga

Dvina

N O R T H   E U R O P E A N   P L A I N

Elbe

Oder

Vistula

Sudeten Mountains

Carpathian Mts.

Dnestr

Dnieper

Hungarian Plain

Sava

Po

Danube

Dinaric Alps

Adriatic Sea

Apennines

Balkan Mountains

Pindus Mts.

▲ Mount Olympus 2911

Aegean Sea

Rhodes

Crete

Volga Uplands

Central Russian Uplands

Sea of Azov

Black Sea

A S I A

3 Arctic Circle

2

1

20°

40°

17

United Kingdom, Republic of Ireland

The British Isles consist of two main islands, Britain and Ireland, and many smaller ones. There are two separate countries in the British Isles - the United Kingdom and the Republic of Ireland.

The United Kingdom (the UK) is made up of England, Scotland, Wales and Northern Ireland. Although the United Kingdom is the proper name, the country is often called Great Britain or Britain for short. Over the centuries many peoples have come to live in Britain. The first of these were invaders such as the Romans and the Vikings. More recently people have come to Britain from all over the world.

Much of northern and western Britain has a highland landscape, while most of the south and east is lower and flatter. A large area of Scotland is mountainous. Britain's highest peak, Ben Nevis, is in the Scottish highlands. Most of Scotland's population lives in the Central Lowlands, between Glasgow and Edinburgh.

UNITED KINGDOM
Capital: **London**
Area: **244 755 square kilometres**
Population: **57.4 million**
Language: **English**
Money: **Pound**

REPUBLIC OF IRELAND
Capital: **Dublin**
Area: **68 895 square kilometres**
Population: **3.5 million**
Language: **English, Irish**
Money: **Punt**

Much of Wales is high ground, with the Cambrian Mountains stretching from north to south across the country. Most of the country's industry is concentrated in and around the main cities of Cardiff and Swansea.

Most of the lowland, and the most fertile farmland in Britain, is found in the southern and eastern parts of England. South east England is dominated by London, the capital city, which has a total population of almost 7 million. London is the centre of government in the UK as well as being the main business centre in the country.

The headquarters of the government of the UK are the Houses of Parliament on the River Thames in London. The clock in the centre is Big Ben.

The island of Ireland is divided between the Republic of Ireland and Northern Ireland. The mild, damp climate of Ireland makes for rich pasture land, and the farming of cattle and sheep is important. In the Republic of Ireland, 14 percent of the workforce is employed in farming, compared to only 2 percent in the UK.

The landscape around Ballyness Bay in Donegal in the northwest of the Republic of Ireland is typical of that part of the country.

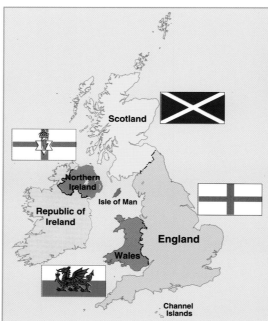

Scotland

Northern Ireland

Isle of Man

Republic of Ireland

England

Wales

Channel Islands

FLAGS OF THE UNITED KINGDOM

The Union Flag is often known as the 'Union Jack'.
The first Union Flag was made in 1606 combining the crosses of St. Andrew of Scotland and St. George of England.

The Flag was altered several times during the next 200 years. In 1801, the saltire of St. Patrick was combined with the crosses of St. Andrew and St. George to form the present 'Union Jack' which is shown on the opposite page.

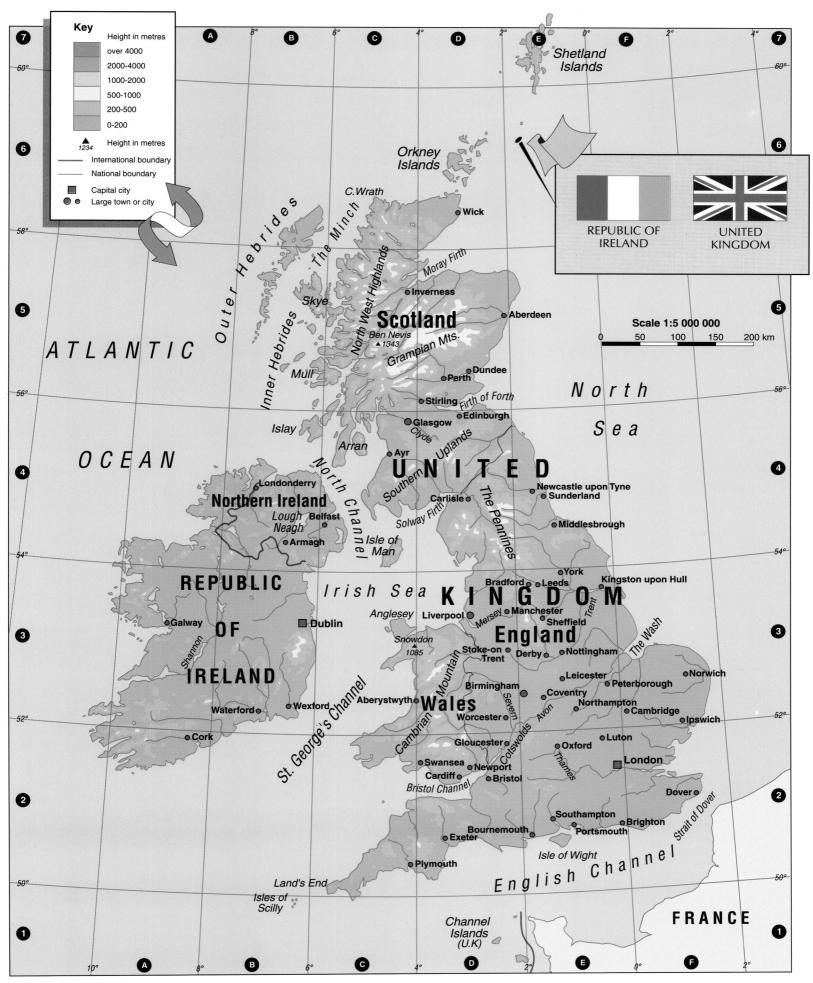

Key

Height in metres

over 4000
2000-4000
1000-2000
500-1000
200-500
0-200

▲
1234   Height in metres

—— International boundary
— National boundary
■ Capital city
● ● Large town or city

REPUBLIC OF IRELAND

UNITED KINGDOM

Scale 1:5 000 000

0   50   100   150   200 km

A T L A N T I C

O C E A N

Outer Hebrides

Inner Hebrides

The Minch

C.Wrath

• Wick

Orkney Islands

Shetland Islands

Skye

North West Highlands

Moray Firth

• Inverness

Scotland

• Aberdeen

Ben Nevis
▲ 1343

Grampian Mts.

Mull

Islay

Arran

• Perth   • Dundee

• Stirling   *Firth of Forth*

• Glasgow   • Edinburgh

Clyde

N o r t h

S e a

• Ayr

Southern Uplands

U N I T E D

• Londonderry

Northern Ireland

Lough Neagh   **Belfast**

• Armagh

North Channel

• Carlisle   *The Pennines*

• Newcastle upon Tyne
• Sunderland

Solway Firth

Isle of Man

• Middlesbrough

K I N G D O M

REPUBLIC

OF

IRELAND

• Galway

■ Dublin

Irish Sea

Shannon

• York

• Bradford   • Leeds   • Kingston upon Hull

Anglesey   • Liverpool   • Manchester

Mersey   • Sheffield

• Stoke-on-Trent   • Derby   • Nottingham   *Trent*

The Wash

England

Snowdon
▲ 1085

• Leicester   • Peterborough   • Norwich

• Waterford   • Wexford

St. George's Channel

• Aberystwyth

Wales

Cambrian Mountain

• Birmingham   • Coventry   • Northampton   • Cambridge

• Worcester   *Severn*   *Avon*   • Ipswich

• Cork

• Gloucester   *Cotswolds*   • Oxford   • Luton

• Swansea   • Newport   • Bristol   *Thames*   ■ London

• Cardiff

Bristol Channel

• Dover

• Southampton   • Brighton   *Strait of Dover*

• Bournemouth   • Portsmouth

• Exeter   *Isle of Wight*

• Plymouth

Land's End

Isles of Scilly

E n g l i s h   C h a n n e l

Channel Islands (U.K)

F R A N C E

Iceland, Norway, Sweden, Finland, Denmark, Estonia, Latvia, Lithuania

In strict geographical terms the name Scandinavia includes only the two countries of Norway and Sweden. Scandinavia is the most northerly part of Europe, and some of the region lies inside the Arctic Circle. The winter climate is very cold, and the Baltic Sea is frozen over for part of the year. On the Atlantic side of Scandinavia the climate is not so cold, as an ocean current of warmer waters, called the North Atlantic Drift, prevents the sea from freezing.

FACTS

DENMARK
Capital: **Copenhagen**
Area: **43 075 square kilometres**
Population: **5.1 million**
Language: **Danish**
Money: **Krone**

ESTONIA
Capital: **Tallinn**
Area: **45 100 square kilometres**
Population: **1.6 million**
Language: **Estonian**   *Money:* **Kroon**

FINLAND
Capital: **Helsinki**
Area: **337 030 square kilometres**
Population: **5.0 million**
Language: **Finnish, Swedish**   *Money:* **Markka**

ICELAND
Capital: **Reykjavik**
Area: **102 820 square kilometres**
Population: **0.3 million**
Language: **Icelandic**   *Money:* **Krona**

LATVIA
Capital: **Riga**
Area: **63 700 square kilometres**
Population: **2.7 million**
Language: **Latvian**   *Money:* **Lat**

LITHUANIA
Capital: **Vilnius**
Area: **65 200 square kilometres**
Population: **3.7 million**
Language: **Lithuanian**   *Money:* **Litas**

NORWAY
Capital: **Oslo**
Area: **323 895 square kilometres**
Population: **4.2 million**
Language: **Norwegian**   *Money:* **Krone**

SWEDEN
Capital: **Stockholm**
Area: **449 790 square kilometres**
Population: **8.6 million**
Language: **Swedish**   *Money:* **Krona**

Norway is a long, narrow and mountainous country. The coast is indented by hundreds of narrow bays, called fjords. Some are more than 100km long, and over 1000m deep. Traditionally Norway has gained its wealth from the sea - from fishing, whaling and shipbuilding, but now the oil industry is very important. Large parts of Sweden are covered in forest, although farming is important in the south. Sweden has major manufacturing industries, and is one of the wealthiest countries in the world.

Denmark is made up of the mainland of Jutland, and a number of islands in the Baltic. Farming is still a major industry in Denmark and bacon, butter, eggs and other farm products are important exports. Most of Finland is covered by forest and lakes - with more than 60 000 lakes in all. Iceland is an island far out in the north Atlantic. The island was formed by the eruption of undersea volcanoes many thousands of years ago.

Despite the ice sheets and glaciers which cover parts of Iceland, there is a lot of volcanic activity on the island. There are many hot springs, volcanoes and geysers. Sometimes violent eruptions light up the sky.

The Baltic States of Estonia, Latvia and Lithuania regained their independence in 1991 when the USSR split up.

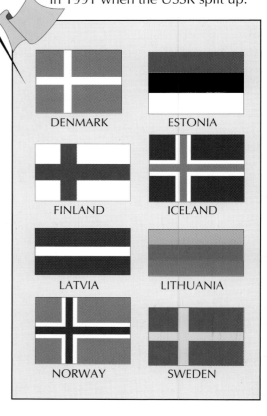

DENMARK   ESTONIA

FINLAND   ICELAND

LATVIA   LITHUANIA

NORWAY   SWEDEN

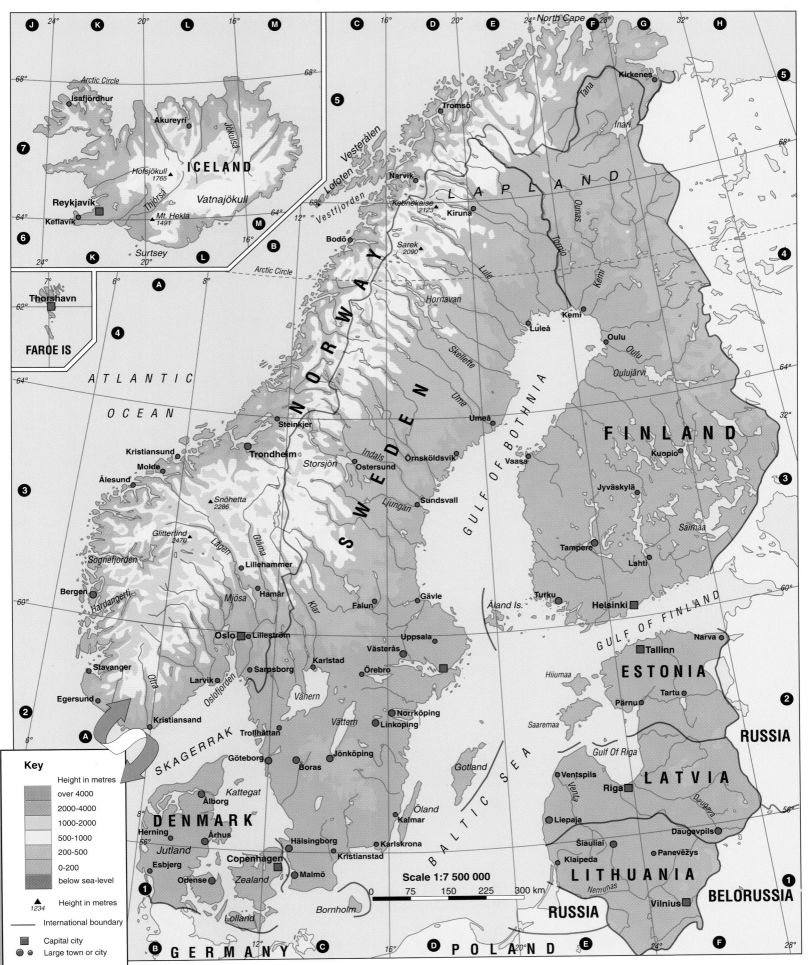

J 24° K 20° L 16° M

68° Arctic Circle 68°

Ísafjördhur

Akureyri

7

Jökulsá

ICELAND

Hofsjökull
1765

Vatnajökull

64° Reykjavík 64°
Keflavík M

Mt. Hekla
1491 B

6 Thjórsá

Surtsey
24° 20°
K L

64°

Thorshavn 7°

62°

FAROE IS

4

A 6° 8°

ATLANTIC

OCEAN

64°

3

Bergen

Hardangerfj.

Sognefjorden

60° Stavanger 60°

Egersund

2 Kristiansand

A 6°

SKAGERRAK

8°

C 16° D 20° E 24° North Cape F 28° G 32° H

5 5

Kirkenes

Tana

Inari

Tromsö

Vesterålen

Lofoten

Narvik

68° Vestfjorden Kebnekaise
2123

Kiruna

LAPLAND

Ounas

Tornio

Kemi

68°

Bodö

Sarek
2090

Lule

Hornavan

Skellefte

Kemi

Luleå

Oulu

Oulu

Oulujärvi

64°

Umeå

Ume

FINLAND

Steinkjer

Kristiansund

Molde

Ålesund

N
O
R
W
A
Y

Trondheim

Storsjön

Indals

Ostersund

Örnsköldsvik

Vaasa

Kuopio

Snöhetta
2286

S
W
E
D
E
N

Ljungan

Sundsvall

Jyväskylä

32°

3

Glittertind
2470

Lågen

Glåma

Lillehammer

Saimaa

Tampere

Lahti

Mjösa

Hamår

Klar

Falun

Gävle

Åland Is.

Turku

Helsinki

60°

Oslo Lilleström

Uppsala

Västerås

Örebro

GULF OF BOTHNIA

GULF OF FINLAND

Narva

Tallinn

Laryik

Sarpsborg

Oslofjorden

Karlstad

Vänern

ESTONIA

Hiiumaa

Pärnu

Tartu

2

Egersund

Otra

Vättern

Norrköping

Linkoping

Saaremaa

Gulf Of Riga

RUSSIA

Trollhättan

Göteborg

Boras

Jönköping

Gotland

Ventspils

LATVIA

Key

Height in metres

over 4000

2000-4000

1000-2000

500-1000

200-500

0-200

below sea-level

▲ Height in metres
1234

— International boundary

◼ Capital city

● ● Large town or city

Ålborg

Kattegat

Herning

DENMARK

Jutland

Esbjerg

56°

Copenhagen

Odense Zealand

1

Lolland

B 12°

GERMANY

Hälsingborg

Århus

Öland

Kalmar

Karlskrona

Kristianstad

Karlstad

BALTIC SEA

Venta

Riga

Daugava

Liepaja

Daugavpils

Šiauliai

Panevėžys

56°

Klaipeda

LITHUANIA

Scale 1:7 500 000

0 75 150 225 300 km

Bornholm

C 16° D 20°

POLAND

Vilnius

Nemunas

RUSSIA

60°

2

RUSSIA

Vingus

BELORUSSIA

E 24° F 28°

21

Netherlands, Belgium, Luxembourg

BELGIUM

LUXEMBOURG   NETHERLANDS

Key

Height in metres

	over 4000
	2000-4000
	1000-2000
	500-1000
	200-500
	0-200
	below sea-level

▲ 1234 Height in metres

——— International boundary

■ Capital city

● ● Large town or city

Scale 1:2 000 000

0   20   40   60   80 km

Belgium, the Netherlands and Luxembourg together are sometimes called the 'Low Countries'. This name comes from the fact that most of the region is very flat and low-lying. The only higher ground is in the south in the hills of the Ardennes.

One third of the Netherlands is so low lying that it is below river and sea levels. Because large rivers, such as the Rhine, flow through the country, flood protection is vital. Earth and stone walls, called dykes, line the rivers and parts of the coast. Since the disastrous floods of 1953, hugely expensive schemes have been built to control the flow of the Rhine and other rivers.

Over the centuries large areas of low lying land have been reclaimed from marshes or from the sea itself. For the last 70 years new farmland, called polder, has been created from the Ijsselmeer, a large lake which was once part of the sea. This reclamation is still going on.

The Netherlands is one of the most densely populated countries in the world. The centre of government is at The Hague, but the two largest cities for industry and business are Amsterdam and Rotterdam. Rotterdam, at the mouth of the river Rhine, is one of the world's largest ports.

▲ The Berlaymont palace in Brussels is the headquarters of the European Union

Belgium became an independent country in 1830. The people of Belgium speak two completely different languages. In the south live the Walloons who speak French. In the north the language used is Flemish, which is a form of Dutch. Like the other Benelux countries Belgium was a founder member of the European Union. The capital, Brussels, was chosen as the location of the European Union headquarters.

Luxembourg is one of the smallest European countries. It is 80km long and nowhere more than 50km across, and has a population of around 400 000.

The harbour area of Europort is part of Rotterdam, Holland and is situated beside the busy shipping lanes in the North Sea. It is now one of the largest ports in the world. ▼

FACTS

BELGIUM
Capital: **Brussels**
Area: **30 520 square kilometres**
Population: **9.8 million**
Language: **French, Dutch**   Money: **Franc**

LUXEMBOURG
Capital: **Luxembourg**
Area: **2 585 square kilometres**
Population: **0.4 million**
Language: **Luxembourgian, French, German**
Money: **Franc**

NETHERLANDS
Capital: **Amsterdam**
Area: **41 160 square kilometres**
Population: **14.9 million**
Language: **Dutch**   Money: **Guilder**

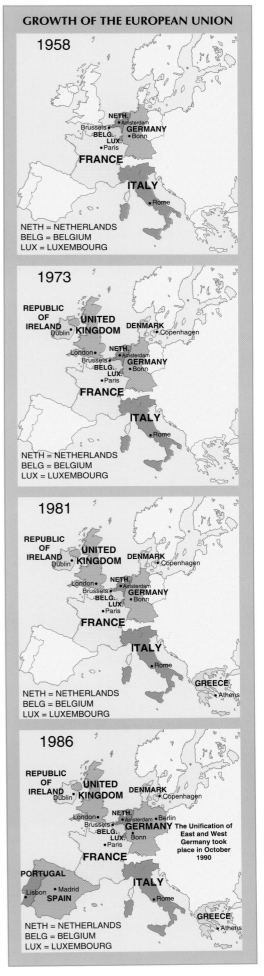

GROWTH OF THE EUROPEAN UNION

1958

NETH = NETHERLANDS
BELG = BELGIUM
LUX = LUXEMBOURG

1973

NETH = NETHERLANDS
BELG = BELGIUM
LUX = LUXEMBOURG

1981

NETH = NETHERLANDS
BELG = BELGIUM
LUX = LUXEMBOURG

1986

The Unification of East and West Germany took place in October 1990

NETH = NETHERLANDS
BELG = BELGIUM
LUX = LUXEMBOURG

France

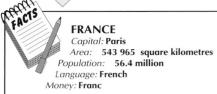

FACTS

FRANCE
Capital: **Paris**
Area: **543 965 square kilometres**
Population: **56.4 million**
Language: **French**
Money: **Franc**

France is the largest country in western Europe. The populations of France and Britain are almost the same, but the land area of France is twice that of Britain.

The north of France has a coastline with the Atlantic Ocean and the English Channel. Southern France lies on the shores of the warm Mediterranean Sea. France has many contrasting landscapes. In Picardy in the north east there are flat farmland areas and industrial towns which developed near coal mines. Further south, in Burgundy, the rolling hills are covered in vines, growing the grapes which make the wine of the area famous worldwide. Further south still, in the heat of Provence farms grow oranges and many other fruits and vegetables.

In contrast, not far from the Mediterranean beaches of the Côte d'Azur, the land rises up to the snow-capped peaks of the Alps. The highest point in the Alps is Mont Blanc (4810m) on the France-Italy border.

Over the centuries France has played a central role in the history of western Europe. The Revolution in the 18th century changed France from being a country ruled by a king, to the republic it is today. The head of state is the president.

The capital of France is Paris, perhaps one of the best-known cities in the world. Located on the river Seine, Paris is famous for its tree-lined boulevards and buildings such as the cathedral of Notre Dame and the palace of the Louvre. A more recent landmark is the Eiffel Tower, built in 1889. Just south of Paris is the huge palace of Versailles, built by King Louis XIV - the 'Sun King'- in the 17th century.

On the south coast of France is Monaco - the smallest independent country in the world - with a land area of only 2.5 square kilometres. Most of this tiny country's wealth comes from tourism. The casinos of Monte Carlo are world famous.

WINE GROWING AREAS

Champagne
Alsace
Loire
Burgundy
Beaujolais
Cognac
Bordeaux
Côte du Rhône
Armagnac
Languedoc
Provence
Roussillon
Corsica

France is world famous for wine. Vineyards, like the one in the photo below, are found in many areas. The type of wine produced depends on the vine best suited to the soil and weather in the region. Famous estates produce and bottle their own wine.

The tiny mountainous country of Andorra lies in the Pyrénees between France and Spain. Most people work on farms or in the tourist industry. Andorra is a popular ski resort.

France has one of the best railway systems in Europe. On some routes, such as Paris to Lyon, high-speed trains (TGV) travel at between 270 and 300km per hour.

FRANCE

Key

Height in metres
- over 4000
- 2000-4000
- 1000-2000
- 500-1000
- 200-500
- 0-200
- below sea-level

▲ 1234   Height in metres

─── International boundary

■ Capital city

● Large town or city

Scale 1:5 000 000

0   50   100   150   200 km

UNITED KINGDOM

English Channel

Channel Islands (U.K)

BELGIUM

GERMANY

LUXEMBOURG

Calais
Boulogne
Roubaix
Lille
Lens
Douai
Valenciennes
Charleville-Méziéres
Thionville
Metz
Somme
Amiens
St. Quentin
Picardy
Cherbourg
Le Havre
Rouen
Beauvais
Reims
Nancy
Strasbourg
Caen
Seine
Oise
Marne
Châlons-sur-Marne
Meuse
Versailles
■ Paris
Chartres
Troyes
Mulhouse
Belfort
Brest
St. Brieuc
Rennes
Le Mans
Orléans
Yonne
Burgundy
Dijon
Besancon
Quimper
Lorient
Belle Ile
St. Nazaire
Nantes
Angers
Tours
Bourges
Chalon-sur-Saône
SWITZERLAND
F R A N C E
Châteauroux
Poitiers
Saône
Ile de Ré
La Rochelle
Montlucon
Mt. Blanc
4810 ▲
Ile d'Oléron
Limoges
Clermont Ferrand
Lyon
Chambéry
Bay of Biscay
Angoulême
St. Etienne
Isère
Grenoble
ITALY
Périgueux
Massif
Valence
Bordeaux
Dordogne
Central
Rhône
Durance
Mt. Pelat
3053 ▲
Lot
Agen
Tarn
Avignon
MONACO
Adour
Montauban
Nîmes
Nice
Monte Carlo
Provence
Aix-en-Provence
Cannes
Bayonne
Pau
Tarbes
Toulouse
Garonne
Canal du Midi
Béziers
Montpellier
Marseille
Toulon
Côte d'Azur
Narbonne
P y r é n é e s
Perpignan
Mediterranean Sea
ANDORRA
S P A I N

25

Germany, Austria, Switzerland

Key

Height in metres

over 4000
2000-4000
1000-2000
500-1000
200-500
0-200

▲ Height in metres
1234

International boundary

■ Capital city

● ● Large town or city

DENMARK

Sylt

NORTH SEA

Flensburg
Fehmarn
Kiel
Rügen
Rostock
Lübeck
Schwerin
Bremerhaven
Hamburg
Oldenburg
Bremen
Ems
Weser
Elbe
NETHERLANDS
Osnabrück
Hannover
Braunschweig
Magdeburg
Potsdam ■ Berlin
Hildesheim
Münster
Bielefeld
G E R M A N Y
Dessau
Oder
Cottbus
Rhine
Essen
Dortmund
Göttingen
Leipzig
Ruhr
Duisburg
Kassel
Dresden
Elbe
Düsseldorf
Neisse
POLAND
Cologne
Erfurt
Aachen
■ Bonn
Gera
BELGIUM
Zwickau
Saale
Frankfurt
Mosel
Wiesbaden
Mainz
Main
CZECH REPUBLIC
LUXEMBOURG
Trier
Würzburg
Kaiserslautern
Mannheim
Heidelberg
Nürnberg
Saarbrücken
Rhine
Karlsruhe
Regensburg
Bohemian Forest
Stuttgart
Scale 1:5 000 000
0 50 100 150 200 km
FRANCE
Danube
Augsburg
Linz
Danube
SLOVAKIA
Black Forest
Munich
Vienna ■
Freiburg
Inn
Salzburg
Neusiedler See
L. Constance
A U S T R I A
Basel
Zürich
St. Gallen
Dachstein ▲ 2996
Enns
Biel
Aare
LIECHTEN-
Innsbruck
Mur
Jura Mts.
Luzern Vaduz STEIN
A L P S
▲ *Grossglockner* 3798
Graz
Berne ■
Wildspitze ▲ 3774
▲ *Eisenhut* 2441
S W I T Z E R L A N D
Chur
HUNGARY
Lausanne
Jungfrau 4158
Klagenfurt
L. Geneva
Drau
Rhône
SLOVENIA
▲ *Matterhorn* 4479

ITALY
CROATIA

A B C D E F

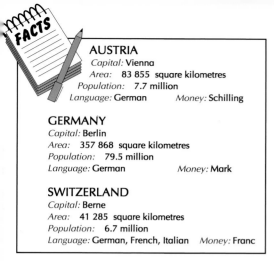

FACTS

AUSTRIA
Capital: **Vienna**
Area: 83 855 square kilometres
Population: 7.7 million
Language: **German**   *Money:* **Schilling**

GERMANY
Capital: **Berlin**
Area: 357 868 square kilometres
Population: 79.5 million
Language: **German**   *Money:* **Mark**

SWITZERLAND
Capital: **Berne**
Area: 41 285 square kilometres
Population: 6.7 million
Language: **German, French, Italian**   *Money:* **Franc**

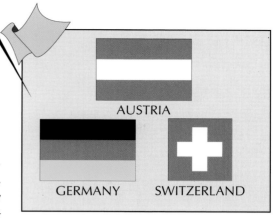

AUSTRIA

GERMANY   SWITZERLAND

Germany, Austria and Switzerland stretch from the North Sea to the Alps. One link between the countries is language - German is spoken throughout Germany and Austria, and by the majority of people in Switzerland.

Germany is the largest of the three countries. At the end of the Second World War it was divided into two separate countries - East Germany and West Germany. The part of Germany that had been occupied by the Russians became the communist country of East Germany. The part that had been occupied by the allied forces from Britain, the USA and France became West Germany. The old German capital of Berlin was now in the East, but the city itself was divided into two, with one half being part of the West although completely surrounded by East German territory. In 1990 the two Germanies were once again united as one country.

Switzerland is a landlocked country. Much of Switzerland is mountainous, and it was in the Swiss Alps that many winter sports such as skiing were first developed. Four languages are used in Switzerland. More than half the people speak German, others speak French or Italian, while a very few people speak a language called Romansch. The Swiss have been neutral in the wars that have affected Europe this century. As a result of this neutrality, Switzerland was made the headquarters of many international organisations, such as the Red Cross.

Austria is another landlocked country. Two thirds of it lies in the mountains of the Alps, although most Austrians live in the lower land around the river Danube. Between Austria and its neighbour, Switzerland, lies the tiny country of Liechtenstein, only 24km long and 8km wide.

The Austrian Alps are very popular for winter sports such as skiing. Cable-cars carry people above the tree-line so they can ski on the higher slopes. ▼

GERMANY'S CHANGING BORDERS
German Empire 1871 - 1918

North Sea — *Baltic Sea*
Hamburg — Danzig
Elbe
Berlin
Rhine — **R u s s i a** — Oder
Frankfurt
Saarbrücken — Prague
Strasbourg
Danube — **A u s t r i a -**
Munich
Salzburg — Vienna — **H u n g a r y**

— German Empire
— Boundary of German Confederation 1815 - 1866

Germany's 1937 borders

North Sea — *Baltic Sea*
Hamburg — Danzig
Elbe
Berlin
Rhine — **P o l a n d** — Oder
Frankfurt
Saarbrücken — Prague
Strasbourg — **Czechoslovakia**
Danube
Munich
Salzburg — Vienna

Austria

— German border

Germany after the Second World War

North Sea — *Baltic Sea*
Soviet admin
Hamburg — Danzig — Polish admin
Elbe
British Zone — Berlin — Under Polish admin
Soviet Zone — **P o l a n d**
Rhine — Oder
French Zone — Frankfurt
American Zone — Prague
Strasbourg — **Czechoslovakia**
French Zone — Danube
Munich
Salzburg — Vienna

Austria

— Germany's 1937 borders
■ Western zones including West Berlin
■ Soviet zones including East Berlin
■ German territories under Polish or Soviet admin

Spain, Portugal

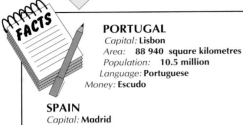

PORTUGAL
Capital: Lisbon
Area: **88 940** square kilometres
Population: **10.5 million**
Language: **Portuguese**
Money: **Escudo**

SPAIN
Capital: **Madrid**
Area: **504 880** square kilometres
Population: **39.0 million**
Language: **Spanish**   *Money:* **Peseta**

In the south western corner of Europe is the Iberian peninsula, which includes the two countries of Spain and Portugal. The southern tip of Spain is divided from Africa by a narrow 15km wide strip of water - the Straits of Gibraltar - which links the Atlantic Ocean with the Mediterranean Sea. The Balearic islands, Majorca, Minorca and Ibiza are also part of Spain.

For two hundred years the wealth from its New World empire made Spain one of the richest and most powerful countries in Europe. Today Spain is a country which is rapidly becoming more industrialised. Tourism too is important - more tourists visit Spain each year than any other country in Europe.

Huge numbers of sardines are caught off the coast of Portugal. On the Algarve coast, tourist developments threaten the traditional ways of life ▼

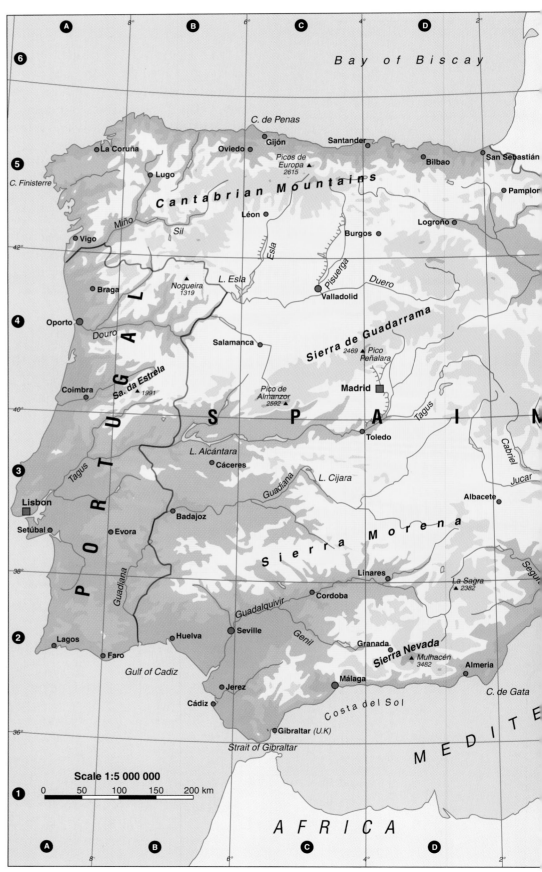

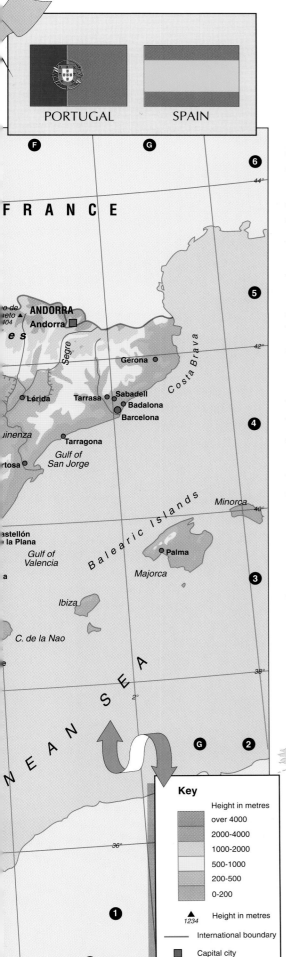

FRANCE

ANDORRA
Andorra □

Segre

Gerona

Lérida   Tarrasa   Sabadell
                      Badalona
                 Barcelona

Tarragona
Gulf of
San Jorge

Costa Brava

Castellón
de la Plana

Gulf of
Valencia

Minorca

Palma

Majorca

Ibiza

C. de la Nao

Balearic Islands

MEAN SEA

Key

Height in metres

	over 4000
	2000-4000
	1000-2000
	500-1000
	200-500
	0-200

▲ Height in metres
1234

—— International boundary
■ Capital city
● ● Large town or city

In many people's minds the picture of Spain may be one of holiday beaches on the Costa del Sol or the Costa Brava. But the tourist beaches are only a tiny part of the real Spain. Much of the country is mountainous, with high upland plateaux and narrow mountain ranges, called sierras. Over the centuries Spain has been invaded by many peoples, including the Romans and the arab Moors from North Africa. The Moors brought with them different styles of building, and great skills in medicine and navigation and left a lasting mark on the country. It was from Spain and Portugal that many of the great sea captain explorers, such as Columbus and Vasco da Gama, set sail on their voyages of discovery. After the exploration of the Americas by Columbus and others, Spain gained a huge empire in the New World. Today Spanish is still the most commonly spoken language in most of South and Central America.

The map below shows the routes of the voyages made by some of the most famous Spanish and Portuguese explorers in the 15th and 16th centuries.

▲ *The Alhambra Palace in Granada in southern Spain was built by the invading arab Moors from north Africa. Its location and fine architecture make it a popular attraction.*

Portugal, Spain's smaller neighbour on the Atlantic coast, also has a history of exploration and empire building. Brazil, the largest country in South America, was once a colony of Portugal, and Portuguese is still the language in Brazil. Today Portugal is one of the poorer members of the European Union countries. Farming is still an important industry. Tourism is becoming a significant part of the economy.

VOYAGES OF DISCOVERY
by the Spanish and Portuguese

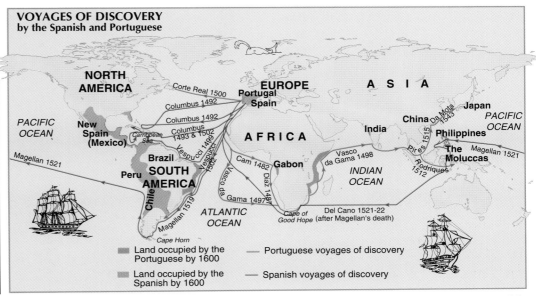

NORTH
AMERICA

EUROPE
Portugal
Spain

ASIA

Corte Real 1500

PACIFIC
OCEAN

New
Spain
(Mexico)

Caribbean
Sea

Columbus 1492

Columbus 1492

Columbus
1493 & 1502

Vespucci 1499

Vespucci 1500

AFRICA

China

Da Mota
1543

Japan

India

PACIFIC
OCEAN

Philippines

Magellan 1521

Pires 1515

The
Moluccas

Magellan 1521

Magellan 1521

Brazil

Peru   SOUTH
        AMERICA

Chile

Cam 1482   Gabon

Vasco da Gama

Diaz 1487

Vasco
da Gama 1498

INDIAN
OCEAN

Rodriques
1512

Gama 1497

ATLANTIC
OCEAN

Cape of
Good Hope

Del Cano 1521-22
(after Magellan's death)

Magellan 1521

Cape Horn

■ Land occupied by the
Portuguese by 1600

■ Land occupied by the
Spanish by 1600

—— Portuguese voyages of discovery

—— Spanish voyages of discovery

Italy

The Rialto Bridge over the Grand Canal in Venice. This beautiful city has been called the 'pearl of the Adriatic', however it faces serious flooding problems.

The boot shape of Italy makes it one of the most easily recognised countries in the world. Italy lies in Southern Europe almost surrounded by the Mediterranean Sea. The two islands of Sicily and Sardinia are also part of Italy.

The capital city of Italy is Rome. Over 2000 years ago Rome was the centre of a great empire which stretched from Britain in the northwest to Egypt in the southeast. The map below shows this empire and some of the names the Romans gave to the cities and regions.

Northern Italy has contrasting landscapes of high mountains and flat plains. The northern border is formed by the Alps. Today the alpine farming has largely given way to tourism, both for winter skiing and for summer holidays by the beautiful lakes. To the south lies the only large, flat region in Italy - the plain of Lombardy. This is the most important region for both farming and industry in Italy. Cities such as Milan, Turin and Bologna are major centres for business and industry.

Central and southern Italy is mainly mountainous. Down the spine of the country is a range of mountains called the Apennines. Most of the larger towns and cities, such as the capital city of Rome, are on the narrow strips of flatter land along the coasts.

The name given to southern Italy is the Mezzogiorno. The difference in wealth between people in the north and south of Italy is striking - the Mezzogiorno is one of the poorest regions in Europe. In recent years there has been development of industry and tourism in the south, but many families still earn their living working on small farms. During the last century many southern Italians, in search of a better life, have migrated to other places - overseas to north America and Australia for example, or north to other parts of Europe, though many are now returning.

The ancient city of Pompeii near Naples was completely buried by an eruption of Mount Vesuvius in 79AD. The ruins are extremely well preserved. ▼

THE ROMAN EMPIRE

Extent of Roman Empire by 31BC

Extent of Roman Empire by 280AD

SWITZERLAND

AUSTRIA

LIECHTENSTEIN

SLOVENIA

CROATIA

YUGOSLAVIA

BOSNIA-
HERZEGOVINA

FRANCE

ITALY

A L P S

Dolomites

Mte. Rosa
▲4634
L. Como
Trento
Udine
Bolzano
Piave
Trieste
Gran Paradiso
▲4061
L. Maggiore
Bergamo
Monza
Brescia
L. Garda
Vicenza
Verona
Padua
Venice
Novara
Milan
Lombardy
Adige
Gulf of
Venice
Turin
Piacenza
Po
Ticino
Alessandria
Mte. Viso
▲3847
Tanaro
Parma
Ferrara
Modena
Genoa
Reggio
Bologna
Ravenna
La Spezia
Mte. Cimone
2165 ▲
Reno
Forlì
Gulf of
Genoa
Rimini

Prato
Arno
Florence
SAN
MARINO
Pisa
A
Arezzo
Ancona
Leghorn
P
LIGURIAN
Siena
e
SEA
L. Trasimeno
n
Perugia
Elba
n
L. Bolsena
i
Terni
Mte. Corno
▲2914
ADRIATIC SEA
Bastia
n
Corsica
(France)
e
Civitavecchia
Tiber
s
Ajaccio
Rome

Str. of Bonifacio

Foggia

Olbia
Benevento
Bari
Sássari
Caserta
Naples
Vesuvius ▲
Salerno
Brindisi
Bradano
Potenza
Táranto
Sardinia
(Italy)
Tirso
T Y R R H E N I A N
Gulf of
Taranto
Str. of Otranto
Oristano
Mte. Pollina
2248 ▲

S E A

Cagliari
Cosenza

Catanzaro
I O N I A N
Stromboli ▲
SEA
Lipari Is.

M E D I T E R R A N E A N
Messina
Palermo
Reggio
Trapani
Nebrodi Mts.
Mt. Etna
▲ 3340
Str. of Messina
S E A
Marsala
S i c i l y
Catania
Agrigento
Salso
Caltagirone
Siracusa
A F R I C A
Ragusa

MALTA
Valletta

Scale 1:5 250 000

0   50   100   150   200 km

FACTS

ITALY
Capital: **Rome**
Area: **301 245 square kilometres**
Population: **57.7 million**
Language: **Italian**
Money: **Lira**

Key

Height in metres
over 4000
2000-4000
1000-2000
500-1000
200-500
0-200

▲   Height in metres
1234

International boundary

■   Capital city
●   Large town or city

31

Slovenia, Croatia, Bosnia-Herzegovina, Yugoslavia, Macedonia, Albania, Romania, Bulgaria, Greece

The countries shown on this map form a region often known as the Balkans. Over the centuries this part of Europe has had a turbulent history having been invaded and fought over many times. The oldest country in the region is Greece. One of the world's first great civilisations grew up in ancient Greece. In the ten centuries before the birth of Christ, the people living in ancient Greek cities developed advanced forms of architecture and government, and great skills in mathematics, medicine and other sciences. The most important city was Athens, now the capital of modern Greece. Greece is the only Balkan country which is a member of the European Union.

Albania is a small country that has remained isolated from the rest of the world for forty years. Today things are slowly changing, and links are being made, but Albania remains the poorest country in Europe.

Romania and Bulgaria both have coastlines on the Black Sea. Their common border lies along the river

FACTS

ALBANIA
Capital: **Tirana**
Area: **28 750 square kilometres**
Population: **3.3 million**
Language: **Albanian**
Money: **Lek**

BOSNIA-HERZEGOVINA
Capital: **Sarajevo**
Area: **51 130 square kilometres**
Population: **4.2 million**
Language: **Serbo-Croat**
Money: **Dinar**

BULGARIA
Capital: **Sofia**
Area: **110 910 square kilometres**
Population: **9.0 million**
Language: **Bulgarian**
Money: **Lev**

CROATIA
Capital: **Zagreb**
Area: **56 540 square kilometres**
Population: **4.6 million**
Language: **Serbo-Croat**
Money: **Dinar**

GREECE
Capital: **Athens**
Area: **131 985 square kilometres**
Population: **10.1 million**
Language: **Greek**
Money: **Drachma**

MACEDONIA
Capital: **Skopje**
Area: **25 713 square kilometres**
Population: **2.034 million**
Language: **Macedonian**
Money: **Dinar**

ROMANIA
Capital: **Bucharest**
Area: **237 500 square kilometres**
Population: **23.2 million**
Language: **Romanian**
Money: **Leu**

SLOVENIA
Capital: **Ljubljana**
Area: **20 250 square kilometres**
Population: **1.9 million**
Language: **Slovene**
Money: **Tolar**

YUGOSLAVIA
Capital: **Belgrade**
Area: **127 885 square kilometres**
Population: **10.0 million**
Language: **Serbo-Croat**
Money: **Dinar**

Danube. In recent years Romania and Bulgaria have seen great changes and the old communist governments have been swept aside.

Tourism is now one of the most important industries in Greece. On the island of Crete many old towns and fishing villages are full of tourists in the summer months.

Key

Height in metres

	over 4000
	2000-4000
	1000-2000
	500-1000
	200-500
	0-200

▲ Height in metres
1234

— International boundary

◼ Capital city

●● Large town or city

Scale 1:5 250 000

0   50   100   150

ALBANIA

BOSNIA-HERZEGOVINA

BULGARIA

CROATIA

GREECE

MACEDONIA

ROMANIA

SLOVENIA

YUGOSLAVIA

Yugoslavia was formed in 1945, but after the fall of communism some of the former six republics that made up Yugoslavia split away. Slovenia, Croatia and Bosnia-Herzegovina became independent in 1991. The people of Bosnia-Herzegovina are divided into Muslims, Serbs and Croats and the struggle for land has been the most bitter in the conflicts following the break-up of Yugoslavia. Macedonia became independent in 1992.

Tirana, the capital of Albania, was founded in the 17th century by Turks. Isolated for many years, Albania is slowly improving its relations with the rest of Europe.

Poland, Czech Republic, Slovakia, Hungary

DENMARK

LITHUANIA

RUSSIA

Baltic

Sea

Gulf of Gdansk

Slupsk
Kolobrzeg
Koszalin
Gdynia
Gdansk
Elblag
L.Mamry
Suwalki

Szczecin
Stargard
Olsztyn
L. Sniardwy

Pila
Bydgoszcz
Grudziadz
Lomza
Bialystok

Vistula
Narew

BELORUSSIA

Notec
Gorzów Wielkopolski
Poznan
Torun
Wloclawek

GERMANY

Warta
Oder
Żeilona Góra
Kalisz
Lódz
Warsaw
Siedlce

P O L A N D

Bug
Wieprz

Legnica
Piotrków Trybunalski
Radom
Lublin

Wroclaw
Walbrzych
Pilica
Kielce

Czestochowa
Opole
Sílesia
Vistula
San

Ustí nad Labem
Gliwice
Sosnowiec
Katowice
Cracow
Tarnów
Rzeszów
Przemysl

UKRAINE

Karlovy Vary
Prague
Pardubice
Ostrava
Bielsko Biala

Plzen
CZECH REPUBLIC
Vltava
Olomouc
Zilina
High Tatra Mts.
Ruzomberok
Presov

Jihlava
Brno
Bystrica
S L O V A K I A
Kosice

Morava
Váh

AUSTRIA
Bratislava
Miskolc
Nyíregyháza

Sopron
Györ
Budapest
Tisza
Debrecen

H U N G A R Y

Szombathely
Székesfehérvár
Szolnok

Veszprém
Danube
Kecskemét

L. Balaton

Nagykanizsa
Szekszárd
Szeged
ROMANIA

Pécs

CROATIA
YUGOSLAVIA

Scale 1:5 000 000

0   50   100   150   200 km

CZECH REPUBLIC   HUNGARY

POLAND   SLOVAKIA

Key

Height in metres

over 4000
2000-4000
1000-2000
500-1000
200-500
0-200

▲ Height in metres
1234

—— International boundary

◼ Capital city

● Large town or city

CZECH REPUBLIC
Capital: **Prague**
Area: **78 860** square kilometres
Population: **10.4** million
Language: **Czech** Money: **Koruna**

HUNGARY
Capital: **Budapest**
Area: **93 030** square kilometres
Population: **10.6** million
Language: **Hungarian**
Money: **Forint**

POLAND
Capital: **Warsaw**
Area: **312 685** square kilometres
Population: **38.2** million
Language: **Polish**
Money: **Zloty**

SLOVAKIA
Capital: **Bratislava**
Area: **20 250** square kilometres
Population: **1.9** million
Language: **Slovak**
Money: **Koruna**

▲ Wenceslas Square is in the centre of Prague, the capital city of the Czech Republic. It is famous for the Royal Palace, St Vitus Cathedral and Prague Castle.

▲ The High Tatra Mountains are situated in northern Slovakia. The area is popular with skiers in winter and walkers in summer.

The four eastern European countries of Poland, Czech Republic, Slovakia and Hungary all border the countries that were part of the former USSR. For most of the last half century these countries had very close links with the USSR. They have had communist governments, and most of their trade was with the USSR. Today all four countries are undergoing great changes. Communism as a form of government has been replaced and links with the countries of western Europe have been increased.

The most northern country Poland. The country first became independent over a thousand years ago. Since that time it has had long periods of being ruled by other nations. Modern Poland, with its capital Warsaw, was formed in 1945, at the end of the Second World War. Almost one third of Poles depend on farming for their living, but this number is falling as more industries are developed. The main industrial centres are Gdansk, a port on the Baltic Sea, and the coalfield area in Silesia in the south of the country.

The Czech Republic and Slovakia are landlocked countries. This part of Europe used to be split between two neighbouring countries - Austria and Hungary, which together formed the great Austro-Hungarian empire. At the end of the First World War in 1918, the Austro-Hungarian empire collapsed. Czechoslovakia was formed as a union of two peoples - the Czechs and the Slovaks. In 1992 Czechoslovakia split up again and became two separate countries, the Czech Republic and Slovakia. As well as Czechs and Slovaks, there are also smaller numbers of Hungarians, Poles and Germans living in these two countries.

Hungary to the south of Slovakia is another landlocked country. Much of Hungary lies in the plain of the river Danube. One of the great rivers of Europe. The Danube plain is an area of fertile farmland, and agriculture is an important industry in Hungary. The Danube is also an important routeway, and river barges travel from western Europe through Hungary to the Black Sea.

The capital city of Hungary, Budapest, was formed from the towns of Buda and Pest. It is a city of beautiful architecture located on the Danube. The photograph shows the parliament buildings. ▼

Belorussia, Ukraine, Moldavia

The town of Yalta on the south coast of the Crimea, is a popular Ukrainian health spa and holiday resort on the Black Sea.

The three new countries of Belorussia, Ukraine and Moldavia were formerly part of the USSR and became independent in 1991 when the USSR broke up. They lie in eastern Europe and apart from the Ukraine are landlocked. To the south the Ukraine is bordered by the Black Sea. The river Dnieper flows south through both Belorussia and Ukraine into the Black Sea.

The largest of the countries is the Ukraine. It lies on a vast plain with the Carpathian Mountains in the extreme south west and mountains on the Crimea peninsula. There are many different types of landscape - marshes, forests, wooded and dry treeless plains. The Ukraine has mild winters and hot summers. The population is mainly Roman Catholic and Orthodox Christian. There is heavy industry in the south, particularly coal mining, iron and steel. On the Black Sea coast there are ship building, chemical and engineering industries. Farming is important on the very fertile 'black earths'. The main crops are wheat, cotton, flax and sugar beet.

Moldavia is the smallest of the three countries but the most densely populated. It lies along the northeast border of Romania. Many Moldavians with a Romanian background would like to join with neighbouring Romania. Moldavia is a land of hilly plains. The river Dniester flows through the west of the country serving as a link with the Black Sea. The soil is fertile and farming is very important especially fruit and market gardening. There is a growing machine building and engineering industry.

The most northerly of the three countries, Belorussia is mainly flat with many lakes and marshes, but when the land is drained it is very fertile. Farming is important. Grain, sugar beet and potatoes are grown and cattle are reared for meat and diary products. Since independence, Belorussian industry has found it difficult to modernise and many factories have had to close.

Belorussia's capital city, Minsk, is over 900 years old. It is an industrial centre and since World War II many high rise flats have been built to house factory workers.

BELORUSSIA
Capital: **Minsk**
Area: **208 000 square kilometres**
Population: **10.3 million**
Language: **Belorussian**
Money: **Rouble**

MOLDAVIA
Capital: **Kishinev**
Area: **33 700 square kilometres**
Population: **4.4 million**
Language: **Romanian**
Money: **Rouble**

UKRAINE
Capital: **Kiev**
Area: **603 700 square kilometres**
Population: **51.9 million**
Language: **Ukrainian, Russian**
Money: **Karbovanets**

Kiev, the capital city of the Ukraine is famous as a cultural and industrial centre. St. Andrew's Cathedral is an example of the city's fine architecture.

Key

Height in metres

	over 4000
	2000-4000
	1000-2000
	500-1000
	200-500
	0-200

▲ Height in metres
1234

— International boundary

◼ Capital city

● Large town or city

Scale 1:7 500 000

0   75   150   225   300 km

LITHUANIA
RUSSIA
POLAND
SLOVAKIA
HUNGARY
ROMANIA
RUSSIA

B E L O R U S S I A
U K R A I N E
M O L D A V I A

Baltic Sea
Black Sea
Sea of Azov
Crimea

Vitebsk
Orsha
Borisov
◼ Minsk
Hrodno
Neman
Baranovichi
Bobruysk
Brest
Pripet
Gomel
Chernigor
Lutsk
Chernobyl
Sumy
Rovno
◼ Kiev
Lvov
Kharkov
Donets
Khmelnitskiy
Kremenchug Reservoir
Vinnytsya
Cherkassy
Kremenchug
Kramatorsk
Lugansk
Kolomyia
Dniester
Kirovograd
Dnepropetrovsk
Gorlovka
Dniester
Donetsk
Beltsy
Krivoy Rog
Zaporozhye
Nikopol
◼ Kishinev
Mariupol
Prut
Tiraspol
Nikolayev
Kakhovka Reservoir
Melitopol
Bendery
Dnieper
Kherson
Odessa
Kerch
Simferopol'
Sevastopol'

37

Countries

ARCTIC OCEAN

RUSSIA

EUROPE

RUSSIA

Moscow

Black Sea

Yakutsk

Omsk
Novosibirsk
Irkutsk
Harbin

KAZAKHSTAN

Ankara
GEORGIA
Tbilisi
ARMENIA
Yerevan
AZERBAIJAN
AZ
Baku
TURKEY
CYPRUS
LEBANON
SYRIA
Damascus
Amman
JORDAN
Baghdad
Tehran
IRAQ
IRAN
Isfahan
KUWAIT
Kuwait City

Caspian Sea
Aral Sea
UZBEKI-STAN
Tashkent
TURKMENISTAN
Ashkabad
Dushanbe
TAJIKISTAN
Alma-Ata
Bishkek
KIRGHIZIA

Ürümqi

Ulan Bator
MONGOLIA
Shenyang
NORTH KOREA
Pyongyang
JAPAN
Tokyo
Sapporo

Beijing
Seoul
SOUTH KOREA
Kobe
Osaka
Fukuoka

Tianjin

Lanzhou
Shanghai

CHINA

Wuhan

Kabul
AFGHANISTAN
Islamabad

SAUDI
BAHRAIN
QATAR
UNITED ARAB EMIRATES
Riyadh
ARABIA
Muscat
OMAN

PAKISTAN
Karachi

New Delhi
NEPAL
Kathmandu
BHUTAN

INDIA
Kanpur
Calcutta
BANGLA-DESH
Dhaka
Mandalay
BURMA (MYANMA)
Yangon

Chongqing

Taibei
TAIWAN
Guangzhou
Kowloon
HONG KONG (U.K.)

Hanoi
LAOS
Vientiane

THAILAND
Bangkok
CAMBODIA
Phnom Penh
VIETNAM
Ho Chi Minh City

PHILIPPINES
Manila

South China Sea

Davao

San'a
YEMEN
Aden

Socotra (Yemen)

AFRICA

Arabian Sea

Bombay
Hyderabad
Madras

Andoman Is. (Ind.)

Nicobar Is. (Ind.)

MALDIVES

SRI LANKA
Colombo

BRUNEI

MALAYSIA
Kuala Lumpur
Singapore
SINGAPORE

SEYCHELLES

INDIAN OCEAN

INDONESIA
Jakarta
Surabaya
Ujung Padang

PACIFIC OCEAN

Tropic of Cancer

Equator

Arctic Circle

Key

— International boundary

■ Capital city

● Other large city

Scale 1 : 45 000 000

0   450   900   1350   1800 km

Landscape

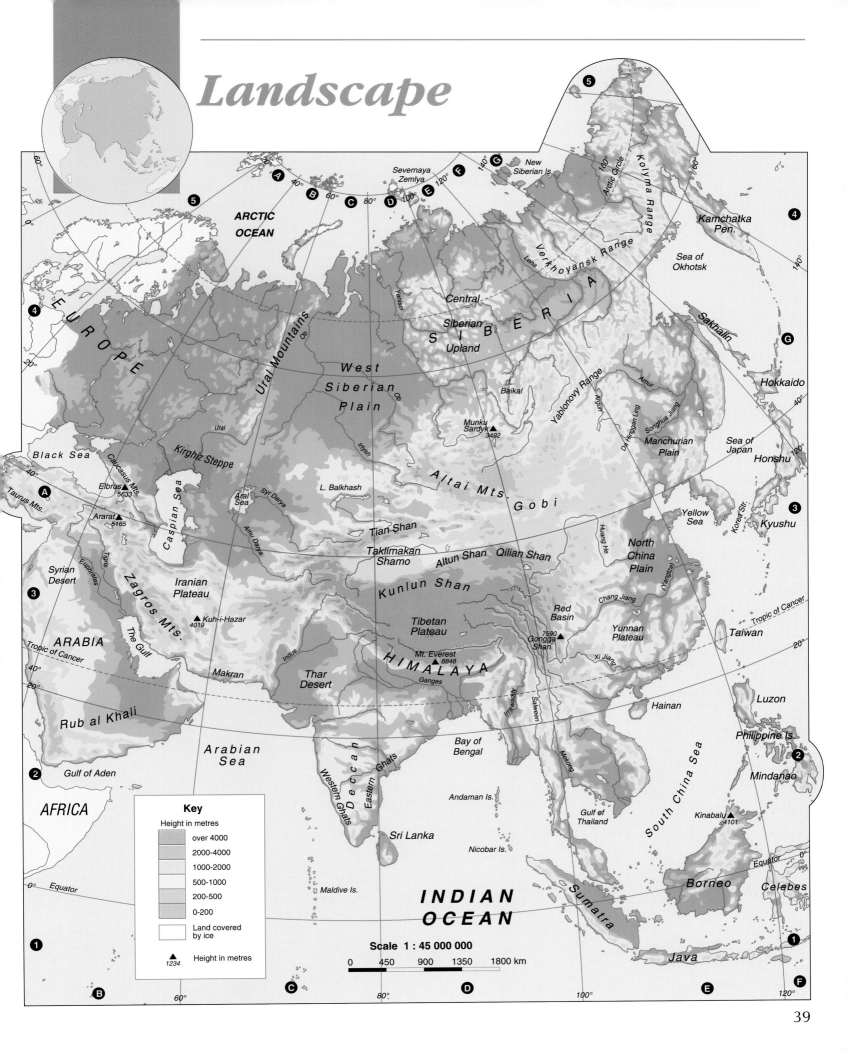

ARCTIC OCEAN

Severnaya Zemlya

New Siberian Is.

Kolyma Range

Kamchatka Pen.

Verkhoyansk Range

Sea of Okhotsk

EUROPE

Central Siberian Upland

S I B E R I A

Sakhalin

Ural Mountains

West Siberian Plain

Ob

Yenisei

L. Baikal

Yablonovy Range

Amur

Hokkaido

Munku Sardyk ▲ 3492

Manchurian Plain

Sea of Japan

Honshu

Black Sea

Kirghiz Steppe

Ural

Irtysh

Altai Mts.

Da Hinggan Ling

Songhua Jiang

Argun

Caucasus Mts.

Elbrus ▲ 5633

Caspian Sea

Aral Sea

Syr Darya

L. Balkhash

G o b i

Yellow Sea

Korea Str.

Kyushu

Taurus Mts.

Ararat ▲ 5165

Amu Darya

Tian Shan

Huang He

North China Plain

Syrian Desert

Tigris

Euphrates

Zagros Mts.

Iranian Plateau

Taklimakan Shamo

Altun Shan

Qilian Shan

Chang Jiang

(Yangtze)

Kuh-i-Hazar ▲ 4019

Kunlun Shan

Red Basin

Yunnan Plateau

ARABIA

The Gulf

Tibetan Plateau

Gongga Shan ▲ 7590

Xi Jiang

Taiwan

Tropic of Cancer

Makran

Indus

Mt. Everest ▲ 8848

H I M A L A Y A

Chang Jiang

Hainan

Luzon

Rub al Khali

Thar Desert

Ganges

Irrawaddy

Salween

Philippine Is.

Arabian Sea

Deccan

Western Ghats

Eastern Ghats

Bay of Bengal

Mekong

South China Sea

Mindanao

Gulf of Aden

Andaman Is.

Gulf of Thailand

Kinabalu ▲ 4101

AFRICA

Sri Lanka

Nicobar Is.

Borneo

Celebes

Equator

Maldive Is.

INDIAN OCEAN

Sumatra

Java

Key
Height in metres

	over 4000
	2000-4000
	1000-2000
	500-1000
	200-500
	0-200
	Land covered by ice
▲ 1234	Height in metres

Scale 1 : 45 000 000

0   450   900   1350   1800 km

39

Russia

Russia is by far the largest country in the world measured by the size of its land. It is so large that it almost circles half way around the world. When it is midday in St Petersburg in the west it is already two hours from midnight on the same day in Vladivostok in the east.

Russia spans two continents - Europe and Asia. Most of the people live in the European part of Russia west of the Ural Mountains, but most of the land lies in Asia. In such a huge country there is a great variety of landscapes and climates. In the north, in Siberia, there are vast areas of tundra and forest where very few people live. To the south, in the plains of the steppe to the west and east of the Ural Mountains, farming is important, especially grain growing. In the southeast around the Black Sea, the climate is sub-tropical, and cotton and vines are grown. The landscape of most of eastern Russia is high plateau and mountains.

The old Russian Empire was ruled by the Tsars (or Emperors). A huge change came with the Revolution in 1917, which threw out the rule of the Tsars and nobles, and brought to power the communists under Lenin, and the Union of Soviet Socialist Republics (the USSR) was formed.

After World War II the USSR became a superpower, but by the late 1980's the old style communism of the Russian Revolution began to make way for newer forms of government which gave people more freedom. In 1991 the USSR broke up and each of the fifteen republics became an independent country.

Today, despite its huge reserves of oil, natural gas, coal, iron ore and many other minerals, Russia is still struggling to modernise its industry and to raise the living standards of its people.

The 12th century buildings of the Kremlin in Moscow include the offices of the government of Russia, as well as St. Basil's Cathedral with its famous domed roofs.

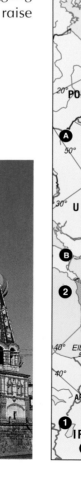

Key

Height in metres

over 4000	▲ Height in metres
2000-4000	*1234*
1000-2000	— International boundary
500-1000	■ Capital city
200-500	● Other large city
0-200	
below sea-level	

The huge grassland plains of Siberia are known as the 'steppes'. This is an area of very fertile soil. Large amounts of cereal crops are grown here. ▶

RUSSIA

FACTS

RUSSIA
Capital: **Moscow**
Area: **17 078 000 square kilometres**
Population: **148.3 million**
Language: **Russian**
Money: **Rouble**

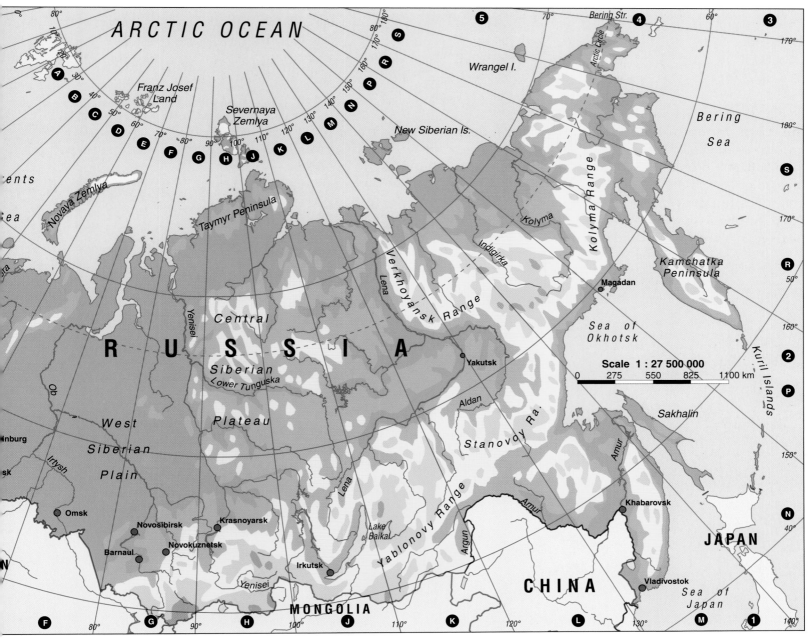

ARCTIC OCEAN

Ⓢ

Ⓐ
Ⓑ
Franz Josef Land
Ⓒ
Severnaya Zemlya
Ⓓ
Ⓔ
Ⓕ Ⓖ Ⓗ Ⓙ Ⓚ Ⓛ Ⓜ Ⓝ Ⓟ Ⓡ

New Siberian Is.

Wrangel I.

Bering Str.
Ⓠ Arctic Circle

Bering Sea

Novaya Zemlya

Taymyr Peninsula

Kolyma Range

Kolyma

Indigirka

Kamchatka Peninsula

Ⓡ
50°

Yenisei

Central

Lower Tunguska

Verkhoyansk Range

Lena

Magadan

Sea of Okhotsk

160°

R U S S I A

Siberian

Plateau

Yakutsk

Aldan

Scale 1 : 27 500 000
0   275   550   825   1100 km

 ②

Ⓟ

West

Ob

Irtysh

Siberian

Plain

Stanovoy Ra.

Sakhalin

Kuril Islands

150°

Ⓝ
40°

Omsk

Novosibirsk

Krasnoyarsk

Lena

Yablonovy Range

Lake Baikal

Amur

Argun

Amur

Khabarovsk

JAPAN

Barnaul

Novokuznetsk

Irkutsk

Yenisei

Vladivostok

Sea of Japan

Ⓕ 80°   Ⓖ 90°   Ⓗ 100°   Ⓙ 110°   Ⓚ 120°   Ⓛ 130°   Ⓜ

MONGOLIA

CHINA

① 140°

Georgia, Armenia, Azerbaijan, Kazakhstan, Uzbekistan, Kirghizia, Tajikistan, Turkmenistan

ARMENIA   AZERBAIJAN   GEORGIA   KAZAKHSTAN

KIRGHIZIA   TAJIKISTAN   TURKMENISTAN   UZBEKISTAN

The eight countries in this region were republics of the former USSR and became independent during 1991 when the USSR broke up. They lie in west central Asia and all, apart from Georgia which borders the Black Sea, are landlocked. Despite its name, the Caspian Sea is a vast inland lake, and is the largest lake in the world.

Scale 1 : 12 500 000
0   125   250   375   500 km

Baku, the capital of Azerbaijan is a port situated on the Caspian Sea. It is an industrial, scientific and cultural centre.

Key

Height in metres

	over 4000
	2000-4000
	1000-2000
	500-1000
	200-500
	0-200
	below sea-level

▲ 1234   Height in metres

—   International boundary

■   Capital city

● ●   Large town or city

The two most westerly countries in this region, Georgia and Armenia, are more European in character and most of the people follow the Orthodox Christian religion. Both countries are mountainous with cold winters and hot summers. The other country in the Caucasus region, on the western shore of the Caspian Sea, is Azerbaijan. In this country many people follow the Muslim religion and the local language, Azerbaijani is related to Turkish.

The largest of the countries to the east of the Caspian Sea is Kazakhstan. The landscape is flat with huge areas of lowlands and plains. Most people are employed in farming but the country is rich in minerals.

The Aral Sea between Kazakhstan and its southern neighbour Uzbekistan used to be the fourth largest lake in the World. Now the Aral Sea is drying up because the water from the rivers that flow into it is used to irrigate crops such as cotton. Over the past thirty years the surface area of the lake has shrunk and towns which used to depend on fishing are now over 60 kilometres from the shore.

To the south of the region lie Turkmenistan and Uzbekistan. Both countries have dry climates with hot summers and cold winters. At one time many people were nomads, herding their animals across the vast grasslands. Now this way of life has almost disappeared. In contrast to the other countries to the east of the Caspian Sea, Tajikistan and Kirghizia are both mountainous.

Lake Ritsa in the Caucasus Mountains in north west Georgia is surrounded by forested mountains which rise to over 3000 metres. ▼

The photograph below is of Rejistan Square in Samarkand, Uzbekistan and shows fine examples of Islamic architecture. ▼

Turkey, Syria, Lebanon, Iraq, Iran, Israel, Jordan, Saudi Arabia, Kuwait, Bahrain, Qatar, United Arab Emirates, Oman, Yemen

The Middle East is a name given to the south western part of the continent of Asia. The name 'Middle East' was first used by Europeans, as this part of the world was not as far east from Europe as other parts of Asia, such as India and China.

In the north the region is bounded by the Caspian Sea, the world's largest lake. The Caspian is famous for its sturgeon fish, from which comes caviar. This northern part is mostly mountainous.

To the south the region becomes flatter, hotter and drier. Almost all of Saudi Arabia is hot desert, including some of the driest areas on earth. The Dead Sea is 80 kilometres long, and 396 metres deep. The sea has a very unusual feature - its surface is 397 metres below sea level. Over thousands of years the River Jordan has flowed into the Dead Sea, bringing with it salt and other minerals, but the level remains the same because water is lost by evaporation. The salt remains, and so over the years the Dead Sea has become very salty. The water is now so thick with salt that a person can easily float almost on the surface of the lake!

▲ *The most famous export from the Middle East is oil. There are huge amounts of oil beneath the ground in places around The Gulf. Countries such as Saudi Arabia, Kuwait, and the United Arab Emirates have grown rich on the money earned from selling their oil to other countries.*

Most of the people in the Middle East are muslims. The holiest place of the Muslim religion is Mecca in Saudi Arabia, the birthplace of the Prophet Muhammad, founder of the religion. Two other major religions have their roots in the region - Christianity and Judaism (the religion of the Jews).

Most of Palestine, the land of the Bible, is now part of the Jewish country of Israel.

Country	Capital City	Area (Sq. Km's)	Population	Language	Money
BAHRAIN	Manama	661	0.5 million	Arabic	Dinar
IRAN	Tehran	1 648 000	54.6 million	Persian	Rial
IRAQ	Baghdad	438 445	18.9 million	Arabic, Kurdish	Dinar
ISRAEL	Jerusalem	20 770	4.7 million	Hebrew	Shekel
JORDAN	Amman	96 000	4.0 million	Arabic	Dinar
KUWAIT	Kuwait City	24 280	2.1 million	Arabic	Dinar
LEBANON	Beirut	10 400	2.7 million	Arabic	Pound
OMAN	Muscat	271 950	1.5 million	Arabic	Rial
QATAR	Doha	11 435	0.5 million	Arabic	Riyal
SAUDI ARABIA	Riyadh	2 400 900	14.9 million	Arabic	Riyal
SYRIA	Damascus	185 680	12.1 million	Arabic	Pound
TURKEY	Ankara	779 450	56.1 million	Turkish	Lira
UNITED ARAB EMIRATES	Abu Dhabi	75 150	1.6 million	Arabic	Dirham
YEMEN	San'a	481 155	11.3 million	Arabic	Rial, Dinar

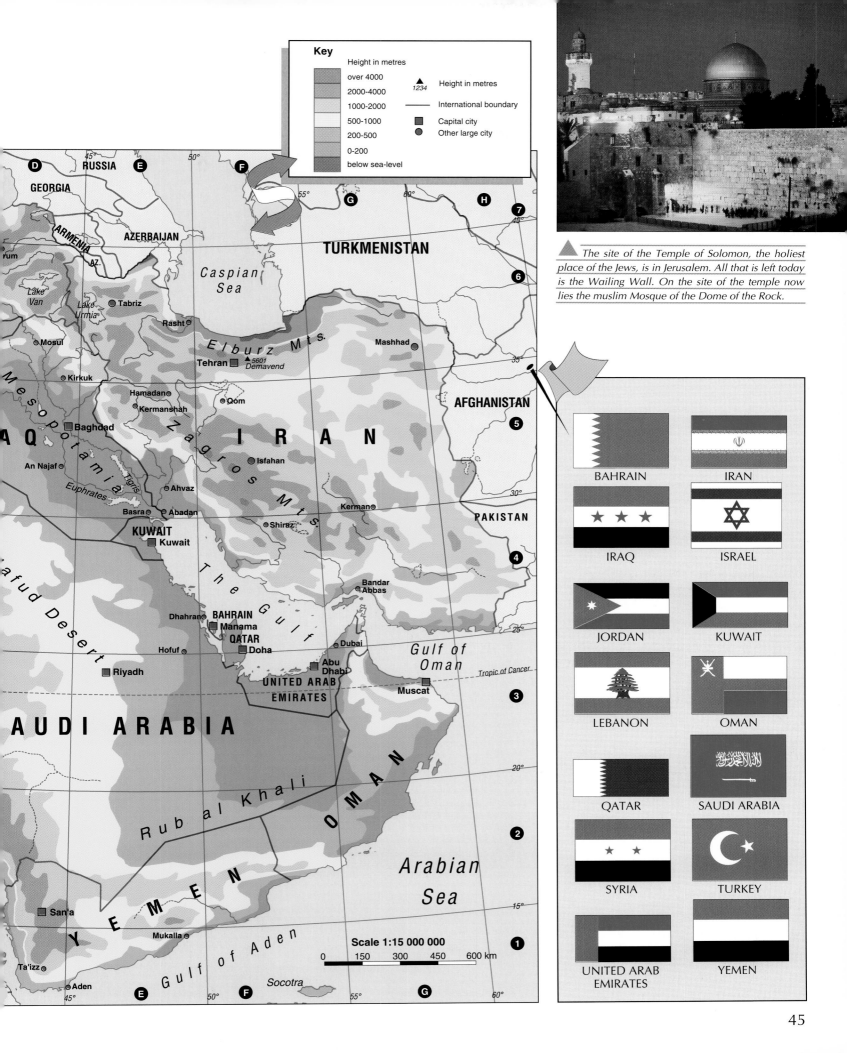

Key

Height in metres

over 4000	
2000-4000	
1000-2000	
500-1000	
200-500	
0-200	
below sea-level	

▲ 1234 Height in metres

— International boundary

■ Capital city

● Other large city

The site of the Temple of Solomon, the holiest place of the Jews, is in Jerusalem. All that is left today is the Wailing Wall. On the site of the temple now lies the muslim Mosque of the Dome of the Rock.

RUSSIA

GEORGIA

ARMENIA

AZERBAIJAN

AZ.

TURKMENISTAN

Lake Van

Lake Urmia

Caspian Sea

Tabriz

Rasht

Elburz Mts.

Mashhad

Mosul

Tehran ▲5601 Demavend

Kirkuk

Hamadan

Kermanshah

Qom

AFGHANISTAN

Baghdad

Mesopotamia

I R A N

Isfahan

An Najaf

Zagros Mts.

Ahvaz

PAKISTAN

Euphrates *Tigris*

Basra Abadan

Shiraz

Kerman

KUWAIT

Kuwait

Bandar Abbas

Nafud Desert

The Gulf

Dhahran BAHRAIN

Manama

QATAR

Hofuf Doha

Dubai

Gulf of Oman

Riyadh

Abu Dhabi

UNITED ARAB EMIRATES

Muscat

Tropic of Cancer

SAUDI ARABIA

O M A N

Rub al Khali

Y E M E N

Arabian Sea

San'a

Ta'izz

Mukalla

Aden

Gulf of Aden

Socotra

Scale 1:15 000 000

0   150   300   450   600 km

Flags

BAHRAIN	IRAN
IRAQ	ISRAEL
JORDAN	KUWAIT
LEBANON	OMAN
QATAR	SAUDI ARABIA
SYRIA	TURKEY
UNITED ARAB EMIRATES	YEMEN

45

Afghanistan, Pakistan, India, Nepal, Bhutan, Bangladesh, Sri Lanka

South Asia is sometimes called the Indian subcontinent, because it almost forms a separate part of the world's largest continent, Asia. South Asia is a fan-shaped area divided from the rest of the continent by a huge chain of mountains - the Himalaya.

South Asia is made up of seven countries - Afghanistan, Pakistan, Bangladesh, Sri Lanka, Bhutan, Nepal, and the largest of them all, India. Between them these countries have a total population of 1000 million - one in five of the world's people.

Key

Height in metres

over 4000	▲ Height in metres
2000-4000	1234
1000-2000	—— International boundary
500-1000	▪ Capital city
200-500	● Other large city
0-200	
below sea-level	

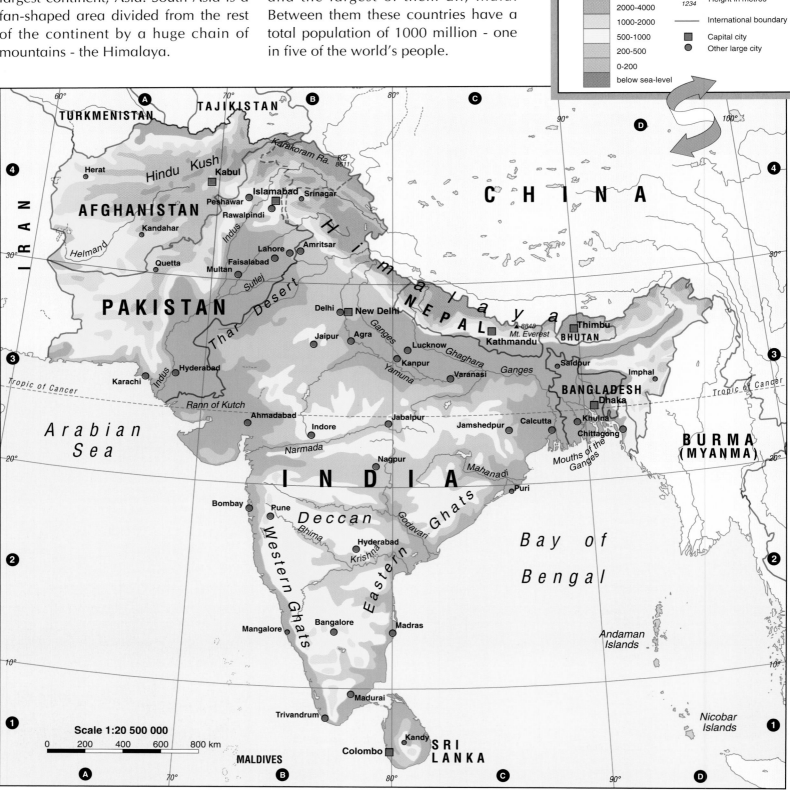

Scale 1:20 500 000

0 200 400 600 800 km

India is a country of almost endless variety - there are many different religions, many different peoples, and over a hundred different languages. Although there are many religions, most people are either muslim or hindu. This was the cause of a serious problem when India gained its independence from Britain in 1947. There are fewer muslims, and they wanted to set up their own country. In the end the country was partitioned, or divided, into what are now known as India, Pakistan and Bangladesh - India is mainly hindu, while the other two countries are mainly muslim.

FACTS

AFGHANISTAN
Capital: **Kabul**
Area: **652 225 square kilometres**
Population: **16.1 million**
Language: **Pushtu, Dari**
Money: **Afghani**

BANGLADESH
Capital: **Dhaka**
Area: **144 000 square kilometres**
Population: **115.6 million**
Language: **Bengali**   *Money:* **Taka**

BHUTAN
Capital: **Thimbu**
Area: **46 620 square kilometres**
Population: **1.5 million**
Language: **Dzongkha**
Money: **Indian Rupee, Ngultrum**

INDIA
Capital: **New Delhi**
Area: **3 166 830 square kilometres**
Population: **827.1 million**
Language: **Hindi, English**   *Money:* **Rupee**

NEPAL
Capital: **Kathmandu**
Area: **141 415 square kilometres**
Population: **18.9 million**
Language: **Nepali**   *Money:* **Rupee**

PAKISTAN
Capital: **Islamabad**
Area: **803 940 square kilometres**
Population: **112.0 million**
Language: **Urdu**   *Money:* **Rupee**

SRI LANKA
Capital: **Colombo**
Area: **65 610 square kilometres**
Population: **17.0 million**
Language: **Sinhalese, Tamil**   *Money:* **Rupee**

▲ *To hindus, the river Ganges in India is sacred. People bathe in the water at special places of pilgrimage.*

▲ *In Bombay, the monsoon season begins in June and over a four month period more than 2 metres of rain falls!*

When Pakistan was founded in the partition of 1947 it had two separate parts over 1000km apart - East Pakistan and West Pakistan. Although the peoples were very different and spoke different languages they were bound together by their religion. But this link could not last for long, and in 1972 East Pakistan broke away and became the independent country of Bangladesh.

South of India lies the island of Sri Lanka, which because of its shape is sometimes called the 'Pearl of the Indian Ocean'.

South Asia, despite its great cities such as Calcutta and Karachi, is still an area where most families earn their living from farming the land. For farmers a reliable supply of water for their animals and crops is vital. In some places, near the rivers, farmers can use irrigation to make sure that there is always water. Elsewhere farmers have to rely on the rain. Almost all the rain in northern and central India and Pakistan comes with what is called the monsoon between the months of May and October. Winds blowing in from the sea bring heavy rains, particularly to the higher ground. In some years the monsoon rains are late, or lighter than usual, and in those years life is hard for the millions of people who depend on their crops of rice and wheat to feed themselves and their families.

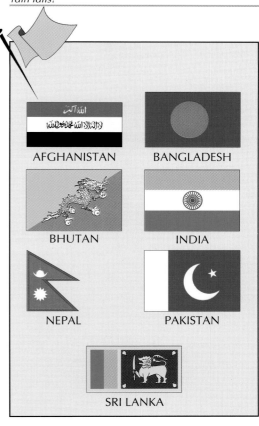

AFGHANISTAN   BANGLADESH

BHUTAN   INDIA

NEPAL   PAKISTAN

SRI LANKA

Mount Everest, in the Himalaya is the world's highest mountain. In fact, the 24 highest peaks in the world are all found in the Himalaya and its neighbouring mountain chains. ▼

Burma, Thailand, Vietnam, Laos, Cambodia, Malaysia, Singapore, Brunei, Philippines, Indonesia

The region of south east Asia is made up of part of the mainland of Asia and the many islands that lie east of India and south of China, between the Indian Ocean and the Pacific Ocean. On the mainland are the countries of Burma, Laos, Cambodia, Vietnam and Thailand (which used to be known as Siam). South of the mainland lie the countries made up of the thousands of islands, large and small, which are dotted across the South China Sea. Malaysia is composed of the narrow peninsula of Malaya and part of the island of Borneo. Indonesia is made up of many islands including Java and Sumatra. The Philippines too is made up of hundreds of islands around the largest island of Luzon.

Singapore city has a skyline dominated by highrise office blocks. Much of the wealth of the tiny country of Singapore comes from trading and manufacturing.

There are two other smaller, but wealthy countries. Singapore has always been an important port and trading centre but it has grown into an important modern manufacturing centre as well. Brunei, a tiny country on the west coast of Borneo is wealthy from its oil.

South east Asia lies across the line of the Equator. The climate here is hot and wet throughout the year. There is very little change from one season to another. The natural vegetation over most of the area is tropical rain forest. In many places it has now been cleared. Some people are very concerned about the speed at which the forest is being cut down, because once cleared, it cannot easily be replaced.

Another change that is coming to parts of south east Asia is the increase in tourism. More people from rich countries in Europe, North America and Japan are visiting the region for their holidays. Facilities for tourists means many changes - more money comes in to help local people, but at the same time traditional ways of life can be changed forever.

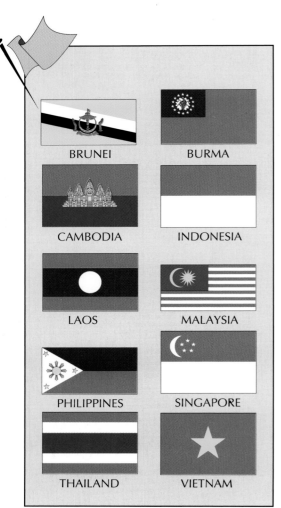

BRUNEI

BURMA

CAMBODIA

INDONESIA

LAOS

MALAYSIA

PHILIPPINES

SINGAPORE

THAILAND

VIETNAM

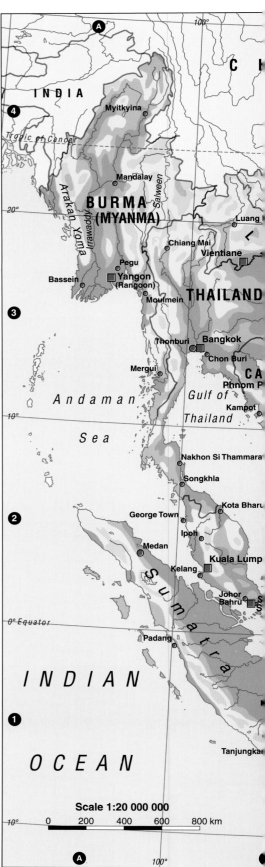

Scale 1:20 000 000

0   200   400   600   800 km

Key

Height in metres

- over 4000
- 2000-4000
- 1000-2000
- 500-1000
- 200-500
- 0-200
- below sea-level

▲ 1234 Height in metres

— International boundary

■ Capital city

● Other large city

During the period of the Khmer Empire, in what is now Cambodia, the great city of Angkor Wat was built. It was abandoned in the 15th century. The ruins show how remarkable the city must have been.

FACTS

BRUNEI
Capital: **Bandar Seri Begawan**
Area: **5 765** square kilometres
Population: **0.3 million**
Language: Malay
Money: **Dollar**

BURMA (MYANMA)
Capital: **Yangon (Rangoon)**
Area: **678 030** square kilometres
Population: **41.7 million**
Language: **Burmes**   Money: **Kyat**

CAMBODIA
Capital: **Phnom Penh**
Area: **181 000** square kilometres
Population: **8.2 million**
Language: **Khmer**   Money: **Riel**

INDONESIA
Capital: **Jakarta**
Area: **1 919 445** square kilometres
Population: **179.3 million**
Language: **Bahasa, Indonesi**   Money: **Rupiah**

LAOS
Capital: **Vientiane**
Area: **236 725** square kilometres
Population: **4.1 million**
Language: **Lao**   Money: **Kip**

MALAYSIA
Capital: **Kuala Lumpur**
Area: **332 965** square kilometres
Population: **17.9 million**
Language: **Bahasa, Malay**   Money: **Ringgit**

PHILIPPINES
Capital: **Manila**
Area: **300 000** square kilometres
Population: **61.5 million**
Language: **Filipino, English**   Money: **Peso**

SINGAPORE
Capital: **Singapore**
Area: **616** square kilometres
Population: **3 million**
Language: **Bahasa Malay**   Money: **Dollar**

THAILAND
Capital: **Bangkok**
Area: **514 000** square kilometres
Population: **57.2 million**
Language: **Thai**   Money: **Baht**

VIETNAM
Capital: **Hanoi**
Area: **329 565** square kilometres
Population: **66.2 million**
Language: **Vietnamese**   Money: **Dong**

HONG KONG

TAIWAN

VIETNAM

Da Nang

Nha Trang

Da Lat

Baguio
San Carlos
Luzon
Quezon City
Manila
PHILIPPINES
Lucena
Mindoro
Samar
Panay
Iloilo
Cebu
Negros
Butuan
Palawan
Iligan
Mindanao
Davao

South China Sea

PACIFIC OCEAN

Sulu Sea

MALAYSIA

Kota Kinabalu
Bandar Seri Begawan
BRUNEI

Celebes Sea

Molucca Sea

Kuching

Borneo

Schwaner Mts

Pegunungan Iran

Kapuas

Balikpapan

Barito

Banjarmasin

Makassar Strait

Manado

Celebes

Ceram Sea

Mamberamo

Maoke Range

Puntjak Jaya ▲ 5030

PAPUA NEW GUINEA

New Guinea

Digoel

Java Sea

Ujung Pandang

INDONESIA

Banda Sea

Aru Is.

Equator

Semarang
Surabaya
Malang
Java
Bali

Flores Sea

Flores

Sumba

Timor

Arafura Sea

49

China, Mongolia, North Korea, South Korea, Taiwan, Hong Kong

China has a larger population than any other country in the world. There are over 1000 million people, which means that one in every five people in the world is Chinese. By land size too China is a huge country. As you would expect in such a large country, there are a great many different landscapes. In the east lie huge cities such as the capital Beijing, Shanghai and Nanjing. Few Chinese own cars but most have bicycles, and one of the images of a Chinese city is of bicycle jams in the rush hours. In contrast to the crowded cities, in the west are the wide open spaces of the Gobi Desert.

For much of its history China has been closed to outsiders. European traders were allowed to settle only in a few places on the coast. The first to come were the Portuguese in 1514, to establish a base at Macau. Later the British colony of Hong Kong was established. Centred first on Hong Kong Island, the colony was given more land in 1898, which could be occupied for 99 years.

In south China lie the bamboo forests of Szechwan, the home of the giant panda. The panda feeds only on a particular type of bamboo, and this is the only location on earth where pandas are found. During this century the number of pandas has declined, and they are now protected. ▼

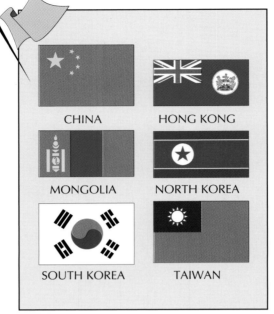

CHINA   HONG KONG

MONGOLIA   NORTH KOREA

SOUTH KOREA   TAIWAN

Hong Kong will become Chinese again in the year 1997. Hong Kong, with its 5 million people, has become an important centre for trade, banking and business.

For most of the first part of this century China suffered from civil war. Finally in 1949 the communists took control of China. The nationalists, who opposed the communists, set up their own country on the island of Taiwan. In the past China did not always grow enough food to feed its huge population. One of the achievements of the present government has been to make sure that all China's people now have enough to eat. Industries too have been developed.

Another country in this region which is divided between communists and non communists is Korea. Once one country, Korea was divided in 1945 at the end of the Second World War. Between 1953 and 1956 a war was fought between the North and the South, but the country still remains divided.

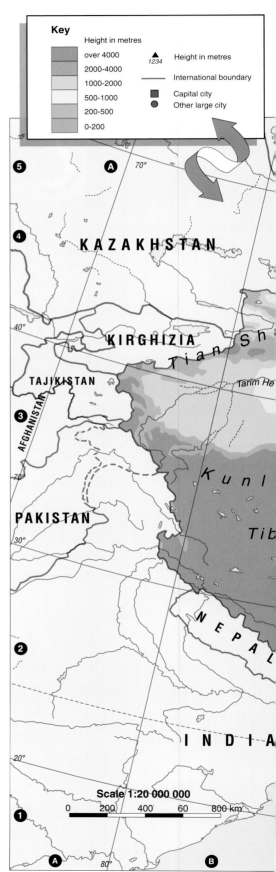

Key

Height in metres

over 4000
2000-4000
1000-2000
500-1000
200-500
0-200

▲ *1234*   Height in metres

International boundary

■ Capital city

● Other large city

Scale 1:20 000 000

0   200   400   60   800 km

CHINA
Capital: **Beijing**
Area: **9 579 000 square kilometres**
Population: **1 139.1 million**
Language: **Mandarin**
Money: **Yuan**

HONG KONG
Capital: **Victoria**
Area: **1 062 square kilometres**
Population: **5.8 million**
Language: **Cantonese, English**
Money: **Dollar**

MONGOLIA
Capital: **Ulan Bator**
Area: **1 565 000 square kilometres**
Population: **2.2 million**
Language: **Khalka, Mongol**
Money: **Tugrik**

NORTH KOREA
Capital: **Pyongyang**
Area: **122 310 square kilometres**
Population: **21.8 million**
Language: **Korean**
Money: **Won**

SOUTH KOREA
Capital: **Seoul**
Area: **98 445 square kilometres**
Population: **42.8 million**
Language: **Korean**
Money: **Won**

TAIWAN
Capital: **Taipei**
Area: **35 990 square kilometres**
Population: **20.3 million**
Language: **Mandarin**
Money: **Dollar**

▲ *The Great Wall of China was built during the Chin Dynasty, 200 years before the birth of Christ, in an attempt to keep out invading armies. Much of it survives today.*

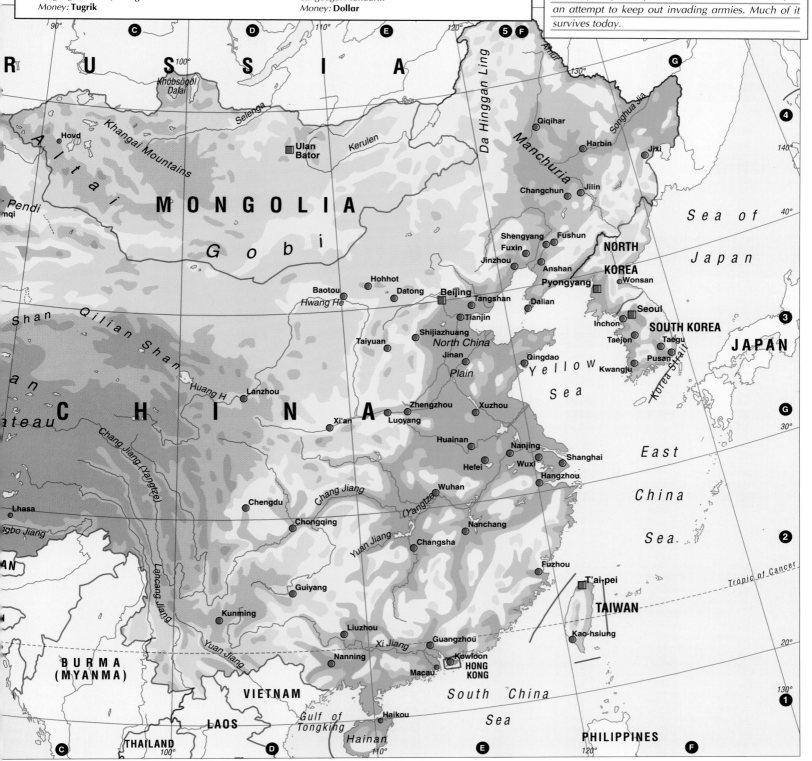

Japan

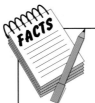

The recent history of Japan is an astonishing one. During this century it has become the greatest industrial country in the world. Japan exports more than any other country - goods ranging from ships, to cars, to electronic equipment and much more. All this has happened despite the fact that Japan has very few natural resources. The country has to import almost all the raw materials needed by Japanese industry.

The country of Japan is made up of four large islands (Honshu, Shikoku, Kyushu and Hokkaido), and over a thousand smaller islands. Much of the country is hilly or mountainous. Most people live on the flat land along the coast. The greatest concentrations of people live near the south coast of Honshu island. The capital city, Tokyo, is one of the world's largest cities.

A high-speed 'bullet train' on its way from Tokyo to Osaka passes the snow-covered peak of Fujiyama. An extinct volcano, Fujiyama is the highest mountain in Japan. ▼

Capital: **Tokyo**
Area: 369 700 square kilometres
Population: 123.5 million
Language: **Japanese**
Money: **Yen**

Japan stretches almost 2000 km from north to south, which means the country has a wide range of different climates. In the south it is warm throughout the year. In the north the island of Hokkaido has cold winters, with temperatures below freezing. Another feature of Japan's climate are the hurricanes or typhoons, which often blow in the late summer.

Today the Head of State of Japan is the Emperor. At one time the Emperor was considered to be a god by many Japanese people. For 600 years, from the 12th century, Japan was ruled by powerful military leaders, called the Shoguns. The armies of the Shoguns were partly made up of a special group of warriors called Samurai. During the years of Shogun rule Japan changed very little, and the country had almost no contact with the outside world.

▲ *The main exports from Japan are electronic and electrical goods. In Tokyo, the night sky is lit-up by neon signs advertising these products.*

NATURAL DISASTERS

Japan has about 70 active volcanoes which erupt frequently, causing loss of life and damage to towns and villages. These volcanoes are part of the 'Ring of Fire' round the Pacific Ocean.

The country also experiences earthquakes, the worst of which was in 1923 near Tokyo when at least 140 000 people died. Earthquakes cause giant tidal waves which can do further damage.

▲ Main Volcanoes

◎ Main earthquakes

∿ Coast liable to tidal waves

Hokkaido
Sapporo ▲Tarumai 1981
◎1952
◎1968
Sea of Japan
Akita
Komaga take ▲1970
1974
Chokai ▲
1964◎
Honshū
▲Azuma 1978
1978
1948◎ ▲Asama Nasu 1977
1991
•Tokyo
1927◎ 1945◎ ◎1923
Kōbe ▲Mihara 1986
Ōsaka ▲Oyama 1983
Shikoku
Aso ▲1991
Unzen 1992 ◎1946
Kyushū
Kirisima 1982
PACIFIC OCEAN

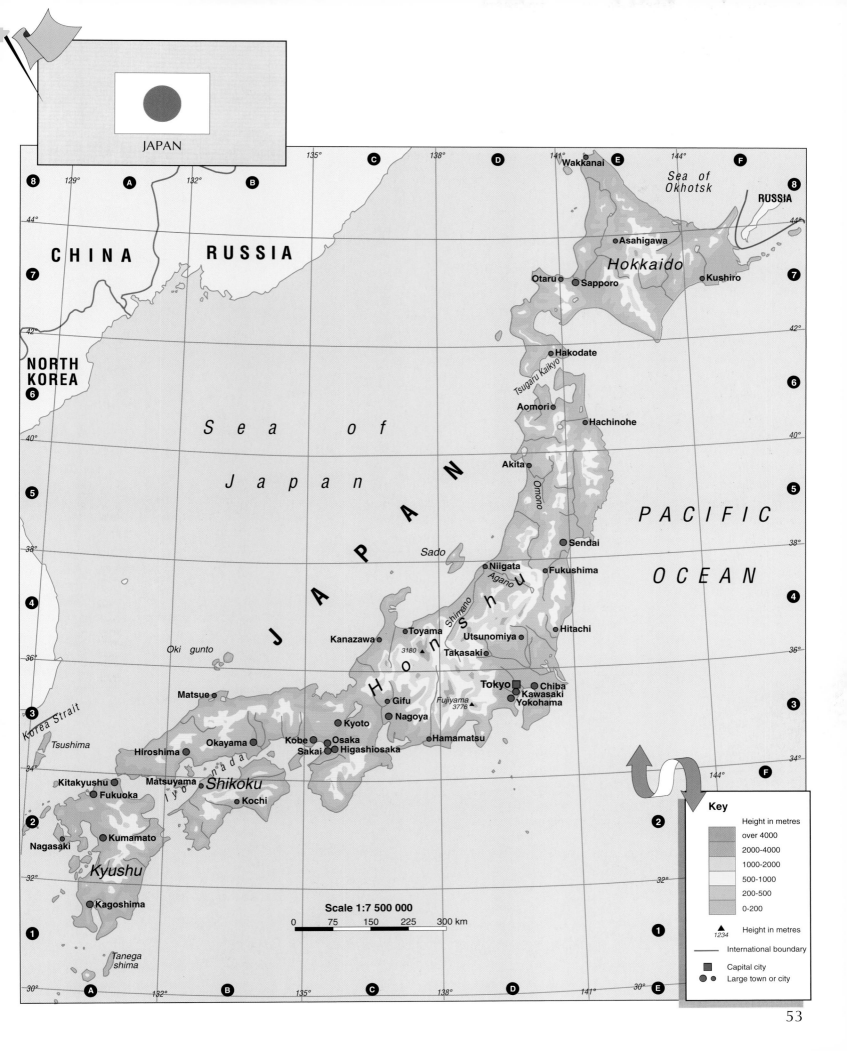

JAPAN

CHINA

RUSSIA

Sea of
Okhotsk

RUSSIA

NORTH
KOREA

Wakkanai

Asahigawa

Hokkaido

Otaru   Sapporo   Kushiro

Hakodate

Tsugaru Kaikyo

Aomori   Hachinohe

Sea   of

Akita

Omono

Japan

PACIFIC

Sendai

Sado   Niigata   Fukushima   OCEAN

Agano

Shinano

Toyama   Utsunomiya   Hitachi
Kanazawa   Takasaki
3180 ▲

Honshu

Oki   gunto

Tokyo   Chiba
Matsue   Gifu   Fujiyama   Kawasaki
3776   Yokohama
Kyoto   Nagoya
Okayama   Kobe   Osaka   Hamamatsu
Hiroshima   Sakai   Higashiosaka

Korea Strait

Tsushima

Iyo nada

Kitakyushu   Matsuyama   Shikoku
Fukuoka   Kochi

Kumamato

Nagasaki

Kyushu

Kagoshima

Scale 1:7 500 000

0   75   150   225   300 km

Tanega
shima

Key

Height in metres

over 4000

2000-4000

1000-2000

500-1000

200-500

0-200

▲ Height in metres
1234

International boundary

■ Capital city

● ●● Large town or city

Countries

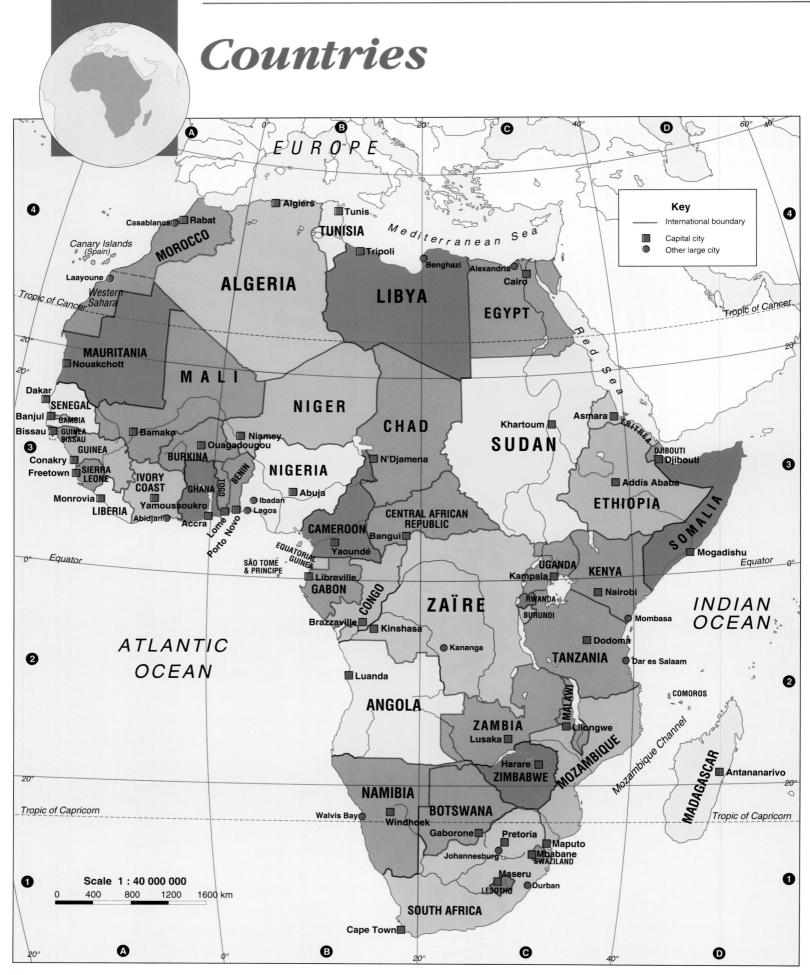

EUROPE

Mediterranean Sea

Key
International boundary
■ Capital city
● Other large city

Algiers
Tunis
TUNISIA
■ Tripoli
Benghazi ●
Alexandria ●
Cairo ■
Casablanca ● ■ Rabat
Canary Islands
(Spain)
MOROCCO
Laayoune ●
Tropic of Cancer
Western
Sahara
ALGERIA
LIBYA
EGYPT
Tropic of Cancer

MAURITANIA
■ Nouakchott
M A L I
NIGER
CHAD
Khartoum ■
Asmara ● **ERITREA**
SUDAN

Dakar ●
SENEGAL
Banjul ●
GAMBIA
Bissau ●
GUINEA-BISSAU
■ Bamako
Niamey ●
Ouagadougou ■
BURKINA
N'Djamena ●
DJIBOUTI
Djibouti ■
GUINEA
Conakry ●
Freetown ●
SIERRA LEONE
IVORY COAST
GHANA
TOGO
BENIN
NIGERIA
Abuja ■
Addis Ababa ●
Monrovia ●
Yamoussoukro ■
LIBERIA
Abidjan ●
Accra ■
Lomé
Porto Novo
Ibadan ●
Lagos ●
CENTRAL AFRICAN REPUBLIC
Bangui ■
ETHIOPIA
SOMALIA
CAMEROON
Yaoundé ■
EQUATORIAL GUINEA
SÃO TOMÉ & PRINCIPE
Libreville ■
GABON
CONGO
UGANDA
Kampala ■
KENYA
Nairobi ●
Mogadishu ●
Equator
Equator
ZAÏRE
RWANDA
BURUNDI
Mombasa ●
Brazzaville ■
Kinshasa ■
Kananga ●
Dodoma ■
INDIAN OCEAN
ATLANTIC OCEAN
Luanda ■
TANZANIA
Dar es Salaam ●
COMOROS
ANGOLA
MALAWI
ZAMBIA
Lilongwe ■
Lusaka ■
MOZAMBIQUE
Harare ■
ZIMBABWE
MADAGASCAR
Antananarivo ■
Mozambique Channel
NAMIBIA
Walvis Bay ●
Windhoek ■
BOTSWANA
Tropic of Capricorn
Tropic of Capricorn
Gaborone ■
Pretoria ■
Maputo ■
Johannesburg ●
Mbabane ■
SWAZILAND
Maseru ■
Durban ●
LESOTHO
SOUTH AFRICA
Cape Town ●

Scale 1 : 40 000 000
0 400 800 1200 1600 km

Landscape

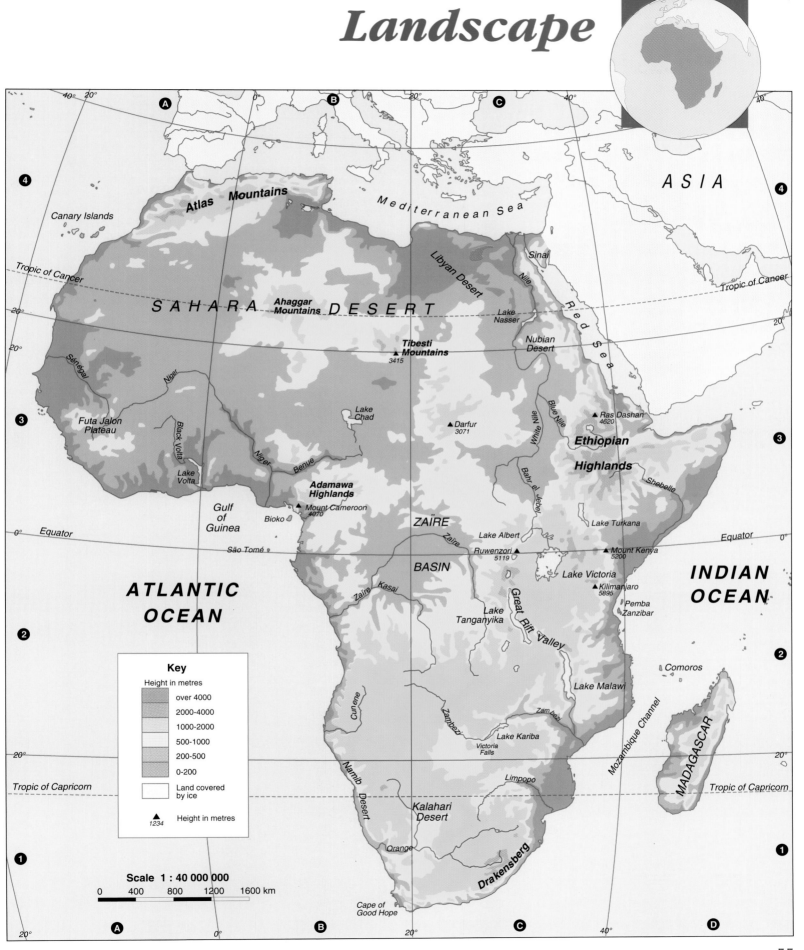

ASIA

Atlas Mountains

Canary Islands

Mediterranean Sea

Tropic of Cancer

Sinai

Libyan Desert

Nile

Lake Nasser

Red Sea

Tropic of Cancer

S A H A R A   D E S E R T

Ahaggar Mountains

▲ Tibesti Mountains
3415

Nubian Desert

Sénégal

Niger

Lake Chad

▲ Darfur
3071

White Nile

Blue Nile

▲ Ras Dashan
4620

Futa Jalon Plateau

Black Volta

Niger

Benue

Bahr el Jebel

Ethiopian Highlands

Lake Volta

Adamawa Highlands

Shebelle

Gulf of Guinea

▲ Mount Cameroon
4070

Bioko

ZAÏRE

Lake Albert

Lake Turkana

Equator

São Tomé

Ruwenzori ▲
5119

▲ Mount Kenya
5200

Equator

BASIN

Zaïre

Lake Victoria

INDIAN OCEAN

ATLANTIC OCEAN

Zaïre   Kasai

▲ Kilimanjaro
5895

Pemba
Zanzibar

Lake Tanganyika

Great Rift Valley

Comoros

Cunene

Lake Malawi

MADAGASCAR

Zambezi

Zambezi

Mozambique Channel

Lake Kariba

Victoria Falls

Tropic of Capricorn

Namib Desert

Limpopo

Kalahari Desert

Tropic of Capricorn

Orange

Drakensberg

Cape of Good Hope

Key

Height in metres

	over 4000
	2000-4000
	1000-2000
	500-1000
	200-500
	0-200
	Land covered by ice

▲ Height in metres
1234

Scale 1 : 40 000 000

0   400   800   1200   1600 km

Morocco, Algeria, Mauritania, Niger, Chad, Sudan, Libya, Egypt, Tunisia, Mali

The largest desert in the world - the Sahara - dominates northern Africa. The Sahara has an area of 9 million square kilometres, and stretches for almost 5000 kilometres from west to east. During the day, temperatures rise as high as 50°C, while at night they can fall as low as freezing. There is very little rainfall.

Most of the people in northern Africa live near the Mediterranean coast or along the banks of the river Nile. The Nile, the world's longest river, brings life to the desert countries through which it flows.

Farming is still important along the Mediterranean coast of northern Africa. Oil is an important source of wealth in Libya, Algeria and Egypt.

To the south of the Sahara Desert lies a region called the Sahel. The Sahel is semi-desert. Recently there have been a number of years when the rainfall has been lower than usual. This has resulted in drought. Crops have failed, and animals have died. Drought has brought hunger and famine, and in some cases death, to the people of the Sahel.

The picture many people have of the Sahara is of sand and dunes. There are 'sand seas' in the desert, but in fact only about fifteen percent of the Sahara is sandy. Most of the desert is rocky or stony.

FACTS

ALGERIA
Capital: **Algiers**
Area: **2 381 745 square kilometres**
Population: **25.0 million**
Language: **Arabic**   *Money:* **Dinar**

CHAD
Capital: **N'Djamena**
Area: **1 284 000 square kilometres**
Population: **5.7 million**
Language: **French, Arabic**   *Money:* **CFA Franc**

EGYPT
Capital: **Cairo**
Area: **1 000 250 square kilometres**
Population: **53.2 million**
Language: **Arabic**   *Money:* **Pound**

LIBYA
Capital: **Tripoli**
Area: **1 759 540 square kilometres**
Population: **4.5 million**
Language: **Arabic**   *Money:* **Dinar**

MALI
Capital: **Bamako**
Area: **1 240 140 square kilometres**
Population: **8.2 million**
Language: **French, Bambara**   *Money:* **CFA Franc**

MAURITANIA
Capital: **Nouakchott**
Area: **1 030 700 square kilometres**
Population: **2.0 million**
Language: **Arabic, French**   *Money:* **Ouguiya**

MOROCCO
Capital: **Rabat**
Area: **446 550 square kilometres**
Population: **25.1 million**
Language: **Arabic**   *Money:* **Dirham**

NIGER
Capital: **Niamey**
Area: **1 186 410 square kilometres**
Population: **7.7 million**
Language: **French**   *Money:* **CFA Franc**

SUDAN
Capital: **Khartoum**
Area: **2 505 815 square kilometres**
Population: **25.2 million**
Language: **Arabic**   *Money:* **Pound**

TUNISIA
Capital: **Tunis**
Area: **164 150 square kilometres**
Population: **8.2 million**
Language: **Arabic**   *Money:* **Dinar**

Key

Height in metres

over 4000	
2000-4000	▲ 1234 Height in metres
1000-2000	—— International boundary
500-1000	■ Capital city
200-500	● Other large city
0-200	
below sea-level	

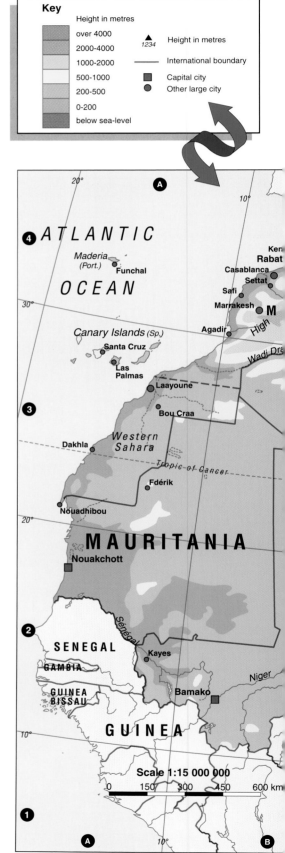

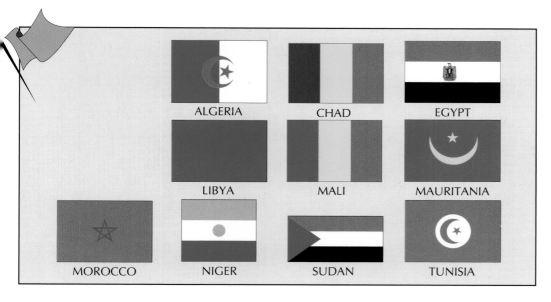

ALGERIA   CHAD   EGYPT

LIBYA   MALI   MAURITANIA

MOROCCO   NIGER   SUDAN   TUNISIA

The cities of Ancient Egypt grew up alongside the Nile. The pyramids and Sphinx at Giza, the temples at Luxor, and the tombs of the pharaohs in the Valley of the Kings can still be seen today.

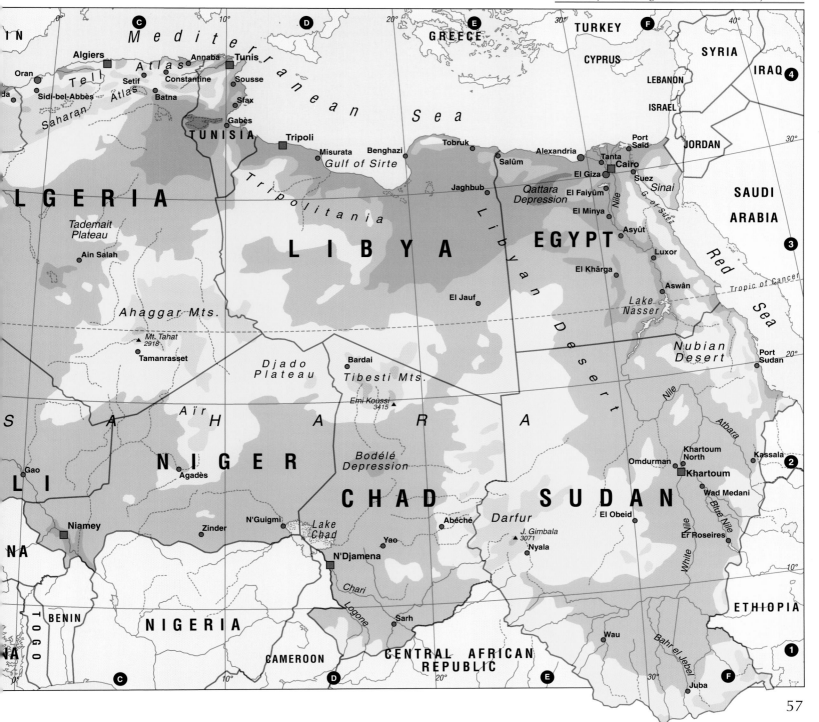

GREECE
TURKEY
CYPRUS
SYRIA
LEBANON
IRAQ
ISRAEL
JORDAN
SAUDI ARABIA

Mediterranean Sea

IN
Algiers
Oran
Annaba
Tunis
Atlas
Tell
Setif
Constantine
Sousse
da
Sidi-bel-Abbès
Atlas
Batna
Sfax
Saharan
Gabès
TUNISIA
Tripoli
Misurata
Benghazi
Tobruk
Salûm
Alexandria
Port Said
Tanta
Cairo
El Giza
Suez
Sinai
Gulf of Sirte
Jaghbub
Qattara Depression
El Faiyûm
Nile
G. of Suez

LGERIA
Tademait Plateau
Tripolitania
LIBYA
EGYPT
El Minya
Asyût
Ain Salah
El Khârga
Luxor
Red Sea
Libyan Desert
El Jauf
Aswân
Tropic of Cancer
Ahaggar Mts.
Lake Nasser
▲ Mt. Tahat 2918
Nubian Desert
Tamanrasset
Port Sudan
Bardai
Djado Plateau
Tibesti Mts.
Nile

S
Aïr
S A H A R A
Emi Koussi ▲ 3415
Atbara
Gao
NIGER
Bodélé Depression
Khartoum North
Kassala
Agadès
CHAD
SUDAN
Omdurman
Khartoum
LI
Wad Medani
NA
Niamey
Zinder
N'Guigmi
Lake Chad
Yao
Abéché
Darfur
El Obeid
J. Gimbala ▲ 3071
Nyala
Er Roseires
Blue Nile
N'Djamena
White Nile
TOGO
BENIN
NIGERIA
Chari
Sarh
Logone
Wau
Bahr el Jebel
ETHIOPIA
CAMEROON
CENTRAL AFRICAN REPUBLIC
Juba

57

Senegal, Gambia, Guinea Bissau, Guinea, Sierra Leone, Liberia, Ivory Coast, Burkina, Ghana, Togo, Benin, Nigeria, Cameroon

On some old maps of Africa, drawn two or three hundred years ago, this region was sometimes called the Slave Coast. It was from West Africa, and particularly the places near the coast, that thousands of African people were sent to North and South America. The people were sent there against their will as slaves. European and Arab slave traders captured them, and had them shipped across the Atlantic to what was called the New World. These people were then sold as cheap labourers for the farms and plantations of Brazil, the West Indies and the southern states of the USA. It was less than two hundred years ago that the West African slave trade was finally stopped.

A sleeping-mat stall at a market in Nigeria. Markets are an important part of West African life

Farming is the most important way of life for people. Subsistence farming is still common, this is where families produce food mainly to feed themselves. Farm products such as rubber, cocoa, palm oil and pineapples are important exports from the region. Other raw materials that are exported from West Africa include oil, diamonds and iron ore. Most of the countries depend heavily on exporting raw materials, to give them the money to import manufactured goods.

By far the largest country in the region is Nigeria. It is four times larger than Britain in area, and it has twice as many people. Once a colony of Britain, Nigeria became independent in 1960. The country is a mix of peoples, in the north most people follow the muslim religion. Ancient cities in the north, such as Kano, have had trading links across the Sahara for centuries. In the south the people are mainly christian or practice local religions.

FACTS

Country	Capital	Area (Sq. Km's)	Population	Language	Money
BENIN	Porto-Novo (de facto)	112 620	4.7 million	French	CFA Franc
BURKINA	Ouagadougou	274 200	9.0 million	French	CFA Franc
CAMEROON	Yaounde	475 500	11.8 million	French English	CFA Franc
GAMBIA	Banjul	10 690	0.9 million	English	Dalasi
GHANA	Accra	238 305	15.0 million	English	Cedi
GUINEA	Conakry	254 855	5.8 million	French	Franc
GUINEA-BISSAU	Bissau	36 125	1.0 million	Portuguese	Peso
IVORY COAST	Yamoussoukro	322 465	12.0 million	French	CFA Franc
LIBERIA	Monrovia	111 370	2.6 million	English	Dollar
NIGERIA	Abuja	923 850	88.5 million	English	Naira
SENEGAL	Dakar	196 720	7.3 million	French	CRA Franc
SIERRA LEONE	Freetown	72 325	4.2 million	English	Leone
TOGO	Lome	56 785	3.5 million	French	CFA Franc

Key

Height in metres
- over 4000
- 2000-4000
- 1000-2000
- 500-1000
- 200-500
- 0-200

▲ 1234 Height in metres

International boundary

■ Capital city

● Other large city

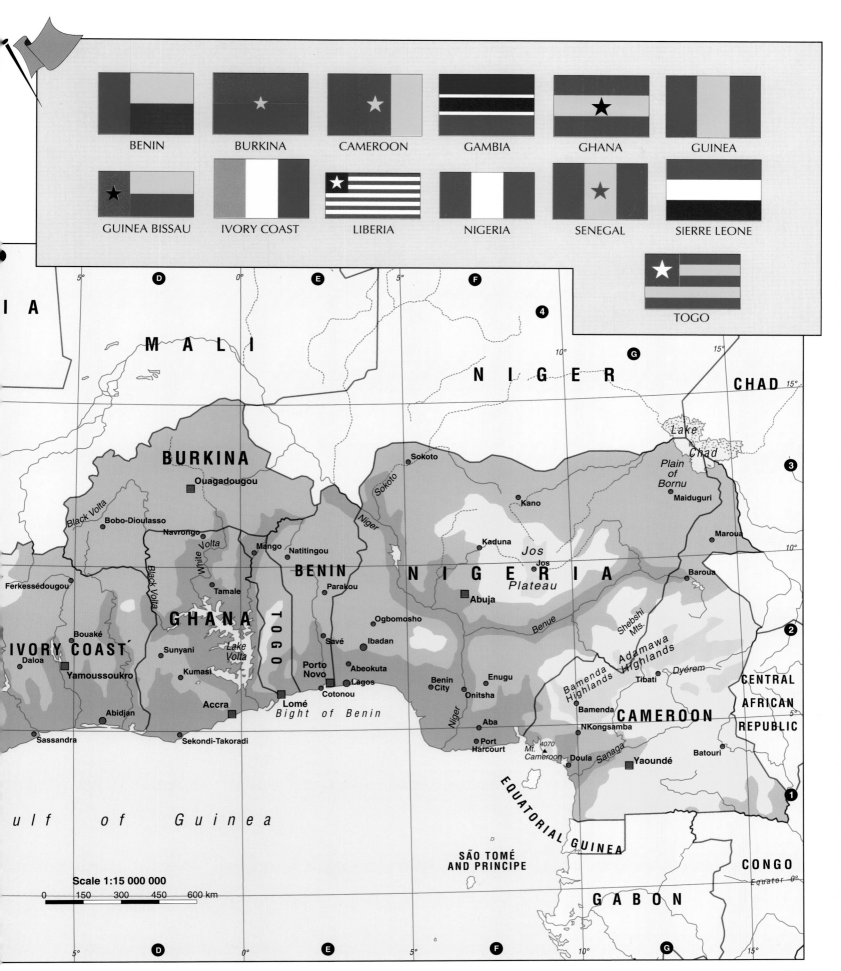

BENIN

BURKINA

CAMEROON

GAMBIA

GHANA

GUINEA

GUINEA BISSAU

IVORY COAST

LIBERIA

NIGERIA

SENEGAL

SIERRE LEONE

TOGO

M A L I

N I G E R

CHAD

BURKINA

Ouagadougou

Black Volta

Bobo-Dioulasso

Navrongo

White Volta

Mango

Natitingou

BENIN

Parakou

N I G E R I A

Sokoto

Sokoto

Niger

Kano

Kaduna

Jos

Jos
Plateau

Lake
Chad

Plain
of
Bornu

Maiduguri

Maroua

Baroua

Ferkessédougou

Tamale

Black Volta

GHANA

Bouaké

Daloa

IVORY COAST

Yamoussoukro

Sunyani

Kumasi

Lake
Volta

T
O
G
O

Savé

Porto
Novo

Abeokuta

Lagos

Cotonou

Ibadan

Ogbomosho

Abuja

Benin
City

Onitsha

Enugu

Benue

Aba

Port
Harcourt

Niger

Shebshi
Mts.

Adamawa
Highlands

Bamenda
Highlands

Tibati

Dyérem

CENTRAL

AFRICAN

REPUBLIC

Accra

Abidjan

Sassandra

Sekondi-Takoradi

Lomé

Bight of Benin

Mt.
Cameroon

4070

Doula

Sanaga

NKongsamba

Bamenda

CAMEROON

Yaoundé

Batouri

G u l f   o f   G u i n e a

SÃO TOMÉ
AND PRINCIPE

EQUATORIAL GUINEA

CONGO

Equator 0°

G A B O N

Scale 1:15 000 000

0   150   300   450   600 km

59

Central African Republic, Equatorial Guinea, Sao Tome and Principe, Gabon, Congo, Zaïre

CENTRAL AFRICAN REPUBLIC

CONGO

EQUATORIAL GUINEA

GABON

SAO TOME & PRINCIPE

ZAÏRE

Located across the equator in the centre of Africa, this region has a climate that is hot and wet throughout the year. Flowing through central Africa are the many rivers which join the great river Zaire (or Congo as it used to be called), before it reaches the Atlantic Ocean.

Over most of the region the natural vegetation is rainforest, or jungle. Parts of the forest have now been cut down, partly to provide land for farmers but mainly to produce hardwood timber for export to richer countries in Europe and North America.

Map

CHAD

SUDAN

CAMEROON

CENTRAL AFRICAN REPUBLIC

Kaga Bandoro
Baboua
Sibut
Carnot
Bangui
Libenge
Bangassou
Monga
Bomu
Uele

Malabo

EQUATORIAL GUINEA

Bata

Principe

SÃO TOMÉ PRINCIPE

São Tomé

Libreville

Zaïre
Aketi
Buta
Isiro
Mungbere
Lisala
L. Albert
UGANDA

Kisangani

Ubundu
L. Edward
Equator

Lambaréné

GABON
CONGO

Sangha

Mbandaka
Basin
ZAÏRE
Lomami

Mbinda

Mai Ndombe

L. Kivu
RWANDA

Bandundu
Kindu
Bukavu
BURUNDI

ATLANTIC OCEAN

Brazzaville

Kasai
Ilebo

Pointe Noire

ANGOLA

Kinshasa
Kitwit

Matadi

Kananga
Mbuji Mayi
Kabalo
Kalemie

Lake Tanganyika

TANZANIA

Lulua

Luvua
Lake Mweru

ANGOLA

Kasai

Lualaba

Dilolo
Kolwezi
Tenke
Likasi
Lubumbashi
ZAMBIA

Key

Height in metres
- over 4000
- 2000-4000
- 1000-2000
- 500-1000
- 200-500
- 0-200

▲ 1234 Height in metres

— International boundary

■ Capital city

● ○ Large town or city

Scale 1:15 000 000

0 150 300 450 600 km

The countries of central Africa do not have large numbers of people. The Central African Republic, for example, is the same size as France, but the population is less than one fifth that of France. The CAR, like all the region's countries, was once a European colony. The CAR became independent of France in 1958. Most people are subsistence farmers, only growing enough food for themselves and their families.

Equatorial Guinea became independent of Spain in 1968. The country is made up of the mainland and five islands in the Atlantic Ocean. Like all the countries in this region, timber is an important export.

Gabon is one of the richer countries in Africa, although the wealth is not shared equally among its population. Its wealth comes from the export of the oil and minerals found in Gabon. The world's largest deposit of the mineral manganese was discovered in this country.

The Congo became independent of France in 1960. The Congo-Ocean railway links the capital Brazzaville with the coast. The railway is a vital transport route, not just for the Congo but also for other countries in central Africa.

The largest country in central Africa is Zaïre, which became independent of Belgium in 1960. This huge country has a relatively small population of under 36 million. In the past this part of Africa suffered very badly from the actions of European and African slave traders. Today Zaire depends heavily on the export of minerals from the Shaba region in the south east of the country.

FACTS

CENTRAL AFRICAN REPUBLIC
Capital: **Bangui**
Area: **624 975 square kilometres**
Population: **3.0 million**
Language: **French, Sango**
Money: **CFA Franc**

CONGO
Capital: **Brazzaville**
Area: **342 000 square kilometres**
Population: **2.3 million**
Language: **French**
Money: **CFA Franc**

EQUATORIAL GUINEA
Capital: **Malabo**
Area: **28 050 square kilometres**
Population: **0.3 million**
Language: **Spanish**
Money: **CFA Franc**

GABON
Capital: **Libreville**
Area: **267 665 square kilometres**
Population: **1.2 million**
Language: **French**
Money: **CFA Franc**

SAO TOMÉ & PRINCIPÉ
Capital: **Sao Tomé**
Area: **964 square kilometres**
Population: **0.01 million**
Language: **Portuguese**
Money: **Dobra**

ZAÏRE
Capital: **Kinshasa**
Area: **2 345 410 square kilometres**
Population: **35.6 million**
Language: **French, Lingala**
Money: **Zaïre**

FUEL AND MINERAL RESOURCES

Around 60% of exports from Zaïre are minerals. Copper mines produce the most important mineral in terms of the country's earnings.

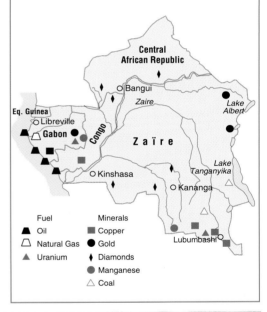

Fuel
▲ Oil
◻ Natural Gas
▲ Uranium

Minerals
◼ Copper
● Gold
◆ Diamonds
● Manganese
△ Coal

Some of the world's valuable rainforests are found in the Congo. In recent years large areas of these have been destroyed to make way for roads and other developments.

Eritrea, Ethiopia, Somalia, Uganda, Kenya, Tanzania, Rwanda, Burundi

In the north of this region, in what is called the Horn of Africa, lie Somalia and Djibouti. Both countries are very hot and dry, and much of Somalia is taken up by desert. To the west and north is Ethiopia and Eritrea. Eritrea was part of Ethiopia until 1993 when it became a separate country. Much of Ethiopia is highland, and so normally receives more rainfall. However, recent dry years in this whole area have resulted in serious droughts and famine for many of the people who make their living from farming crops and cattle.

Further south lie Kenya and Tanzania. Although Kenya lies across the equator, much of the country is higher land and so cooler. On farms and plantations in the highlands crops such as coffee and tea are grown for export. Tanzania gained its name when the country was formed by the joining of what was once the British colony of Tanganyika, with the island of Zanzibar in the Indian Ocean.

The most striking feature of East Africa is the Great Rift Valley. In some places the steep sides of the valley fall over 1000m to the valley floor. Long, narrow lakes - the largest being lakes Turkana, Tanganyika and Malawi - fill many parts of the valley floor.

Tropical grassland, or savanna, covers large parts of Kenya and Tanzania. These are the East African plains where huge game herds still graze. The grazing animals include zebra, elephant, giraffe, wildebeest and many other types of antelope, ostriches, buffalo and rhinoceros. Preying on the grazing animals are the meat eating predators - lion, leopard, cheetah, hyena and jackal. In the past the huge herds moved almost unhindered, migrating with the seasons to follow the rains and fresh grazing. Today the animals have to be protected in game parks, such as the Masai Mara Reserve in Kenya, and the Serengeti Park in Tanzania, shown on the map below. Some animals are in particular need of protection.

BURUNDI
Capital: Bujumbura
Area: 27 834 square kilometres
Population: 5.5 million
Language: **French, Kirundi**
Money: Franc

ERITREA
Capital: Asmara
Area: 93 679 square kilometres
Population: 3.5 million
Language: **Amharic, English** *Money:* **Birr**

ETHIOPIA
Capital: Addis Ababa
Area: 1 221 900 square kilometres
Population: 47.5 million
Language: **Amharic** *Money:* **Birr**

KENYA
Capital: Nairobi
Area: 582 645 square kilometres
Population: 24.0 million
Language: **Swahili, English** *Money:* **Shilling**

RWANDA
Capital: Kigali
Area: 26 330 square kilometres
Population: 7.2 million
Language: **Kinyarwanda, French**
Money: Franc

SOMALIA
Capital: Mogadishu
Area: 630 000 square kilometres
Population: 7.5 million
Language: **Arabic, Somali** *Money:* **Shilling**

TANZANIA
Capital: Dodoma
Area: 939 760 square kilometres
Population: 25.6 million
Language: **Swahili, English** *Money:* **Shilling**

UGANDA
Capital: Kampala
Area: 236 580 square kilometres
Population: 18.8 million
Language: **Swahili, English** *Money:* **Shilling**

WILDLIFE PARKS IN EAST AFRICA

Kabalega Falls National Park
Lake Turkana
Uganda
Kampala
Kenya
Mt. Kenya
Lake Victoria
Masai Mara Reserve
Nairobi
Kigali
Rwanda
Bujumbura
Serengeti Nat. Park
Tsavo National Park
Burundi
Kilimanjaro
Lake
Tanzania
Dodoma
Tanganyika
Ruaha National Park
Selous Game Reserve
Lake Malawi

National Parks and Reserves
Largest Parks named.

In the past fifty years, the number of elephants in East Africa has been dramatically reduced. Large numbers of elephants have been killed by poachers, who sell the tusks for their ivory. Tourists visit the many wildlife parks in East Africa.

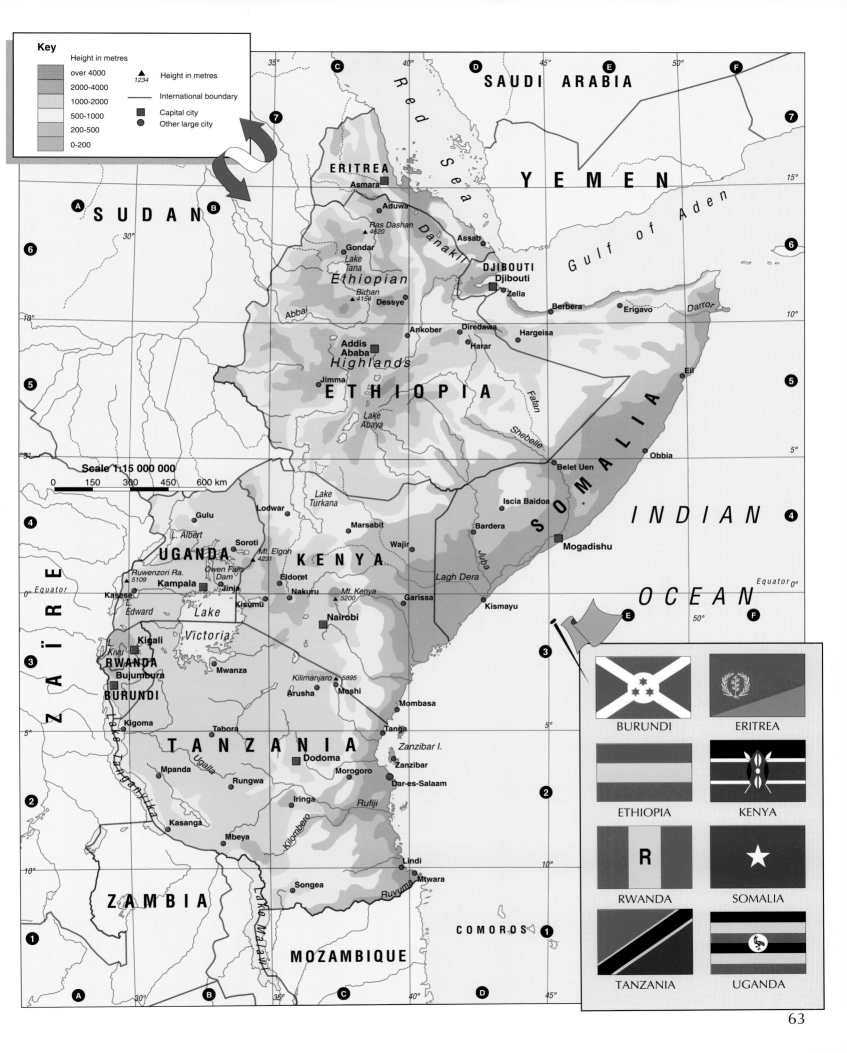

Key

Height in metres

	over 4000
	2000-4000
	1000-2000
	500-1000
	200-500
	0-200

▲ 1234   Height in metres

──   International boundary

■   Capital city

●   Other large city

SAUDI ARABIA

YEMEN

Red Sea

Gulf of Aden

ERITREA

Asmara ■
● Aduwa
▲ Ras Dashan 4620
● Gondar
Lake Tana
Ethiopian

Danakil

● Assab

DJIBOUTI
Djibouti ■
● Zella

● Berbera   ● Erigavo   Darror

▲ Birhan 4154   ● Dessye

Abbai

● Ankober   ● Diredawa   ● Hargeisa
● Harar

Addis Ababa ■
Highlands

● Jimma

ETHIOPIA

Lake Abaya

Fafan

Shebelle

**S
O
M
A
L
I
A**

● Eil

SUDAN

● Obbia

Belet Uen ●

● Iscia Baidoa

INDIAN

Lake Turkana

● Lodwar

● Gulu

● Marsabit

● Bardera

Juba

● Mogadishu ■

Scale 1:15 000 000

0   150   300   450   600 km

L. Albert

● Soroti
Mt. Elgon ▲ 4231

UGANDA

KENYA

Ruwenzori Ra. ▲ 5109
Kampala ■
Owen Falls Dam
● Jinja
● Kasese
L. Edward

● Wajir

Lagh Dera

● Garissa

● Kismayu

Equator

OCEAN

● Eldoret
● Nakuru
● Kisumu
Mt. Kenya ▲ 5200

Nairobi ■

**Z
A
Ï
R
E**

● Kigali ■
RWANDA
L. Kivu
Bujumbura ■
BURUNDI

Lake Victoria

● Mwanza

Kilimanjaro ▲ 5895
● Arusha   ● Moshi

● Mombasa

● Kigoma

● Tabora

TANZANIA

Dodoma ■

● Tanga

Zanzibar I.
● Zanzibar
● Dar-es-Salaam

Lake Tanganyika

● Mpanda

Ugalla

● Rungwa

● Morogoro

● Iringa

Rufiji

● Kasanga

● Mbeya

Kilombero

● Lindi
● Mtwara

ZAMBIA

Lake Malawi

● Songea

Ruvuma

COMOROS

MOZAMBIQUE

BURUNDI	ERITREA
ETHIOPIA	KENYA
RWANDA	SOMALIA
TANZANIA	UGANDA

Angola, Zambia, Malaŵi, Mozambique, Comoros, Madagascar, Zimbabwe, Botswana, Namibia, South Africa, Swaziland, Lesotho

The southern part of the African continent is a region of striking contrasts. In the north east are the lakes that lie in the southern part of the Great Rift Valley. In this part there are tropical grasslands, or savanna, which used to support huge herds of game animals. On the wetter west coast there is tropical rainforest. In contrast, further inland lies the dry expanse of the Kalahari desert. Not much is known about some of the earlier history of the region. An early civilisation developed around the ancient, but now ruined, city of Zimbabwe. This civilisation gave its name to the modern country of Zimbabwe.

The Namib desert stretches along the Atlantic coast of Namibia. Some of the highest sand dunes in the world are found in this area.

At the border between Zambia and Zimbawe on the Zambezi river are the Victoria Falls. The spectacular views of the falls attract many tourists.

The first Europeans to settle in South Africa were the Dutch, who set up a base at the Cape of Good Hope in 1652. By early this century South Africa was a wealthy country, yet this wealth was concentrated into the hands of the white people, and very little reached the black South Africans who made up the largest group of people in the country.

In 1960 the government set up the apartheid (meaning 'living apart') system. Black people did not have the same rights as whites - they could not vote, and could only live in 'black' areas of towns and cities. Today, the apartheid system is being broken up, and all people will have equal rights.

FACTS

Country	Capital	Area (Sq. Km's)	Population	Language	Money
ANGOLA	Luanda	1 246 700	10.0 million	Portuguese	Kwanza
BOTSWANA	Gaborone	600 372	1.3 million	English, Tswana	Pula
COMOROS	Moroni	1 860	0.55 million	Arabic, French	CFA Franc
LESOTHO	Maseru	30 345	1.8 million	English, Sesotho	Loti
MADAGASCAR	Antananarivo	594 180	11.2 million	Malagasy, French	Franc
MALAWI	Lilongwe	94 080	8.3 million	English, Chichewa	Kwacha
MOZAMBIQUE	Maputo	784 755	15.7 million	Portuguese	Metical
NAMIBIA	Windhoek	824 295	1.8 million	Afrikaans, English	Namibian Dollar
SOUTH AFRICA	Cape Town / Pretoria	1 184 825	35.3 million	Afrikaans, English	Rand
SWAZILAND	Mbabane	17 365	0.8 million	English, SiSwati	Emalangeni
ZAMBIA	Lusaka	752 615	7.8 million	English	Kwacha
ZIMBABWE	Harare	390 310	9.4 million	English	Dollar

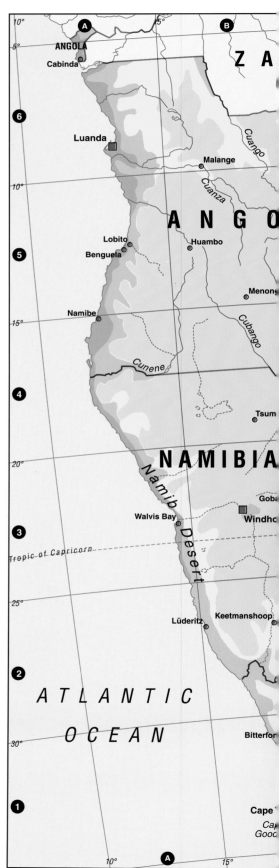

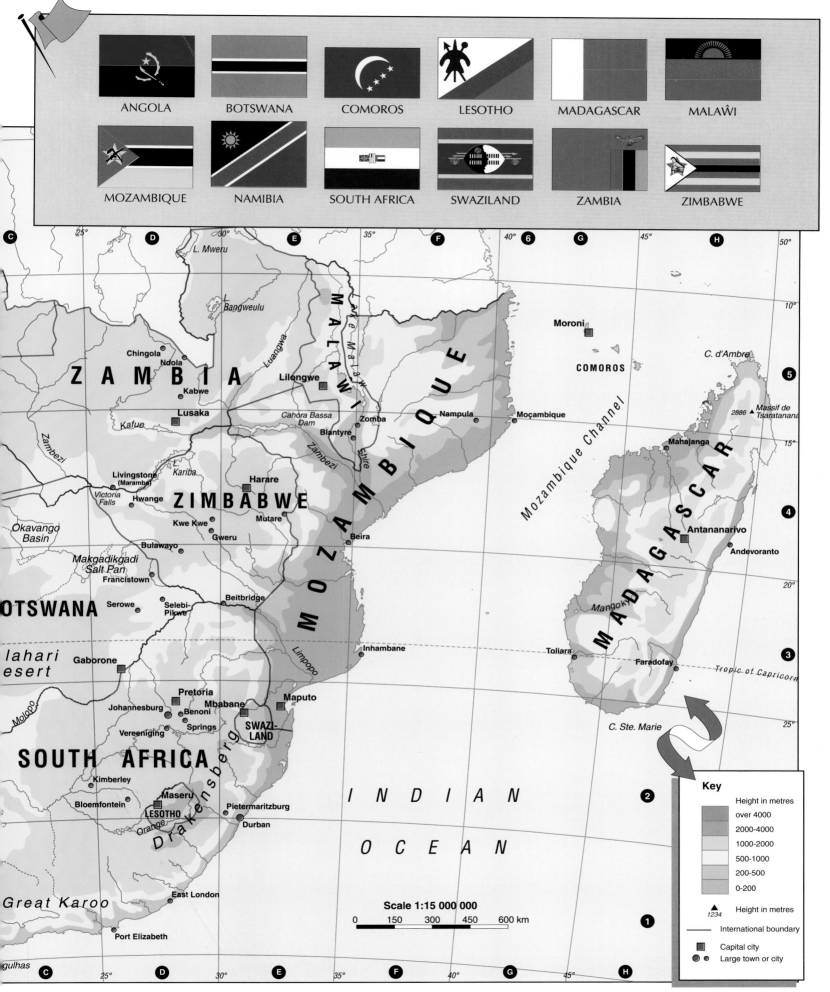

ANGOLA BOTSWANA COMOROS LESOTHO MADAGASCAR MALAŴI

MOZAMBIQUE NAMIBIA SOUTH AFRICA SWAZILAND ZAMBIA ZIMBABWE

25° 30° 35° 40° 45° 50°

L. Mweru

L. Bangweulu

ZAMBIA

Chingola
Ndola
Kabwe
Lusaka
Kafue
Zambezi

Livingstone
(Maramba)
Victoria
Falls
Hwange
Kariba
Okavango
Basin

OTSWANA

Serowe
Selebi-
Pikwe

Gaborone

lahari
esert

Molopo

SOUTH AFRICA

Kimberley
Bloemfontein
Maseru
LESOTHO

Great Karoo

Luangwa

Lilongwe

Cahora Bassa
Dam
Blantyre
Zomba

MOZAMBIQUE

Harare
ZIMBABWE
Kwe Kwe
Gweru
Bulawayo
Mutare
Beira

Makgadikgadi
Salt Pan
Francistown

Beitbridge

Limpopo

Pretoria
Johannesburg
Benoni
Springs
Vereeniging
SWAZI-
LAND
Mbabane
Maputo

Drakensberg

Orange
Pietermaritzburg
Durban

East London

Port Elizabeth

gulhas

MALAŴI
Lake Malaŵi

Shire

Zambezi

Nampula
Moçambique

Inhambane

Moroni

COMOROS

Mozambique Channel

C. d'Ambre

2886 ▲ Massif de
Tsaratanana

Mahajanga

MADAGASCAR

Antananarivo
Andevoranto

Mangoky

Toliara

Faradofay

Tropic of Capricorn

C. Ste. Marie

INDIAN

OCEAN

Scale 1:15 000 000

0 150 300 450 600 km

Key

Height in metres

over 4000
2000-4000
1000-2000
500-1000
200-500
0-200

▲   Height in metres
1234

International boundary

■   Capital city

● ●   Large town or city

65

Countries

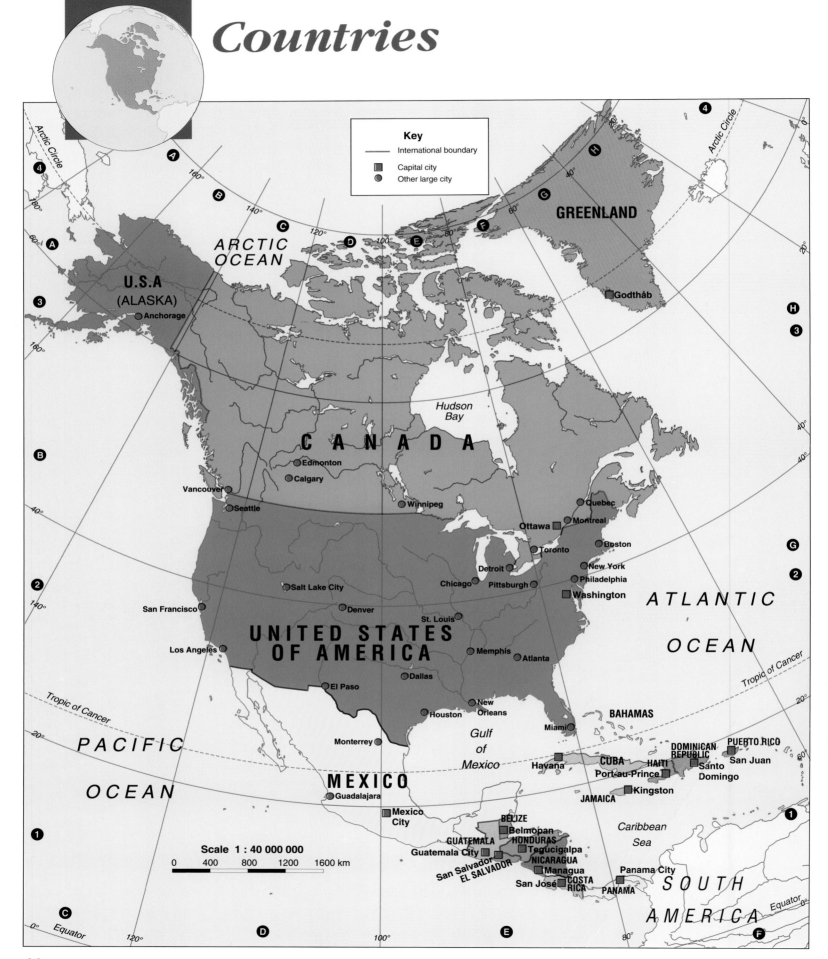

Key

International boundary

▪ Capital city

● Other large city

ARCTIC OCEAN

GREENLAND

U.S.A (ALASKA)

● Anchorage

▪ Godthåb

Hudson Bay

C A N A D A

● Edmonton

● Calgary

● Vancouver

● Seattle

● Winnipeg

● Quebec

▪ Ottawa ▪ Montreal

● Boston

● Toronto

● Detroit ● New York

● Chicago ● Pittsburgh ● Philadelphia

● Salt Lake City ▪ Washington

● San Francisco ● Denver

● St. Louis

UNITED STATES OF AMERICA

● Los Angeles ● Memphis ● Atlanta

● Dallas

● El Paso

● Houston ● New Orleans

● Miami

BAHAMAS

ATLANTIC OCEAN

PACIFIC OCEAN

● Monterrey

Gulf of Mexico

▪ Havana

CUBA

DOMINICAN REPUBLIC

PUERTO RICO

▪ San Juan

HAITI

▪ Port-au-Prince ▪ Santo Domingo

MEXICO

● Guadalajara

JAMAICA

▪ Kingston

Caribbean Sea

▪ Mexico City

BELIZE

▪ Belmopan

GUATEMALA HONDURAS

● Guatemala City ▪ Tegucigalpa

San Salvador NICARAGUA

EL SALVADOR ▪ Managua

San José COSTA RICA

● Panama City

PANAMA

SOUTH AMERICA

Scale 1 : 40 000 000

0   400   800   1200   1600 km

Tropic of Cancer

Equator

Arctic Circle

Landscape

ASIA

ARCTIC OCEAN

GREENLAND

Ellesmere Island

Baffin Bay

Baffin Island

Davis Strait

Bering Strait

Brooks Range

Yukon

Banks Island

Victoria Island

Alaska Range
▲ Mt. McKinley
6194

Kodiak Island

Alaska Pen.

▲ Mt. Logan
6050

Great Bear Lake

Great Slave Lake

Hudson Bay

Labrador

Newfoundland

Mackenzie

Peace

Vancouver Island

Coast Mountains

Churchill

Nelson

Saskatchewan

Albany

Canadian Shield

St. Lawrence

C. Breton Island

R O C K Y

M O U N T A I N S

Columbia

Lake Superior

Lake Huron

Lake Ontario

C. Cod

Lake Michigan

Lake Erie

Missouri

PACIFIC

OCEAN

Coast Range

Great Salt Lake

Great Basin

Platte

▲ Mt. Elbert
4399

Ohio

Tennessee

Appalachian Mts

C. Hatteras

Colorado

Colorado Plateau

Ozark Plateau

Arkansas

Mississippi

ATLANTIC

OCEAN

Red

Tropic of Cancer

Gulf of California

Sierra Madre Occidental

Altiplano Mexicano

Sierra Madre Oriental

Rio Grande

Florida

Bahama Islands

Gulf of Mexico

Cuba

Hispaniola

Lesser Antilles

Greater Antilles

Yucatan Peninsula

Caribbean Sea

5699 ▲

Sierra Madre

SOUTH

AMERICA

Isthmus of Panama

Equator

Key

Height in metres

- over 4000
- 2000-4000
- 1000-2000
- 500-1000
- 200-500
- 0-200
- Land covered by ice

▲ Height in metres
1234

Scale 1 : 40 000 000

0   400   800   1200   1600 km

United States of America

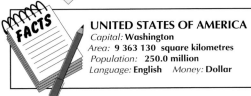

UNITED STATES OF AMERICA
Capital: **Washington**
Area: **9 363 130 square kilometres**
Population: **250.0 million**
Language: **English** *Money:* **Dollar**

The USA is sometimes called just the 'States'. This is because the country is made up of 50 separate states. Forty eight of them are linked together in the area shown on the map. In addition there are two other states - Alaska at the north-western tip of the continent of North America, and the islands of Hawaii in the Pacific Ocean.

The capital city is Washington DC. The 'DC' stands for 'District of Columbia', and means that Washington is not in any one state but in its own special district.

The USA is a country of many different landscapes. In the centre of the country lie the flat lands of the Great Plains, crossed by many rivers. Almost all these rivers eventually join one great river - the Mississippi. The Mississippi, and its main tributary the Missouri, together form the fourth longest river in the world.

The Great Plains were once all grasslands, where huge herds of bison and other animals grazed. Today the land is used for farming. Crops such as wheat and corn are grown, and cattle are raised.

Either side of the Great Plains there are mountains. To the east lie the Appalachians, and to the west are the higher peaks of the Rocky Mountains. West of the Rockies lies the driest part of the USA, the deserts of Nevada and Arizona. Near the west coast lies another mountain range, the Sierra Nevada. In these mountains grow the giant redwood trees, or sequoia, the tallest trees in the world.

In the north east of the country are the Great Lakes, which form part of the USA's border with Canada. The lakes are frozen for three or four months each winter. In contrast, in the south east is Florida, surrounded on three sides by the warm waters of the Caribbean Sea, and visited by holiday makers throughout the year.

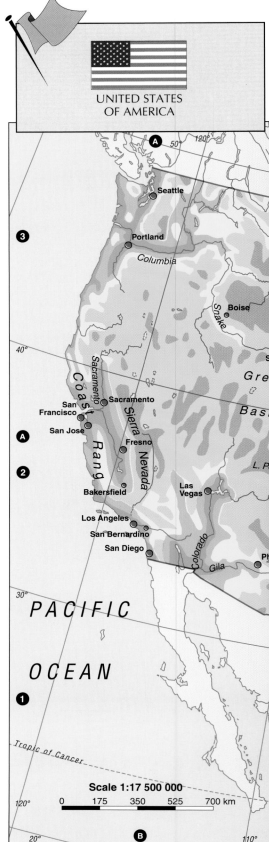

UNITED STATES
OF AMERICA

Scale 1:17 500 000

| 0 | 175 | 350 | 525 | 700 km |

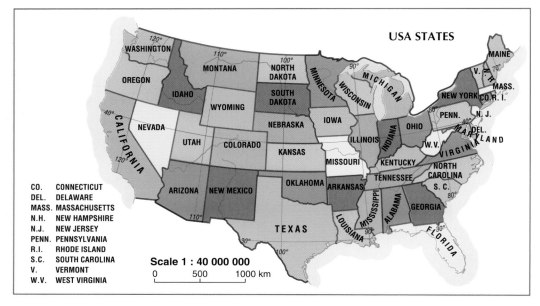

USA STATES

CO. CONNECTICUT
DEL. DELAWARE
MASS. MASSACHUSETTS
N.H. NEW HAMPSHIRE
N.J. NEW JERSEY
PENN. PENNSYLVANIA
R.I. RHODE ISLAND
S.C. SOUTH CAROLINA
V. VERMONT
W.V. WEST VIRGINIA

Scale 1 : 40 000 000

| 0 | 500 | 1000 km |

The Grand Canyon is a huge valley which has been cut a mile deep by the Colorado river. It is an area of beautiful scenery which attracts many visitors.

The Mississippi river flows south towards the Gulf of Mexico. It was used for transport long before roads and railways were built, and is still used today.

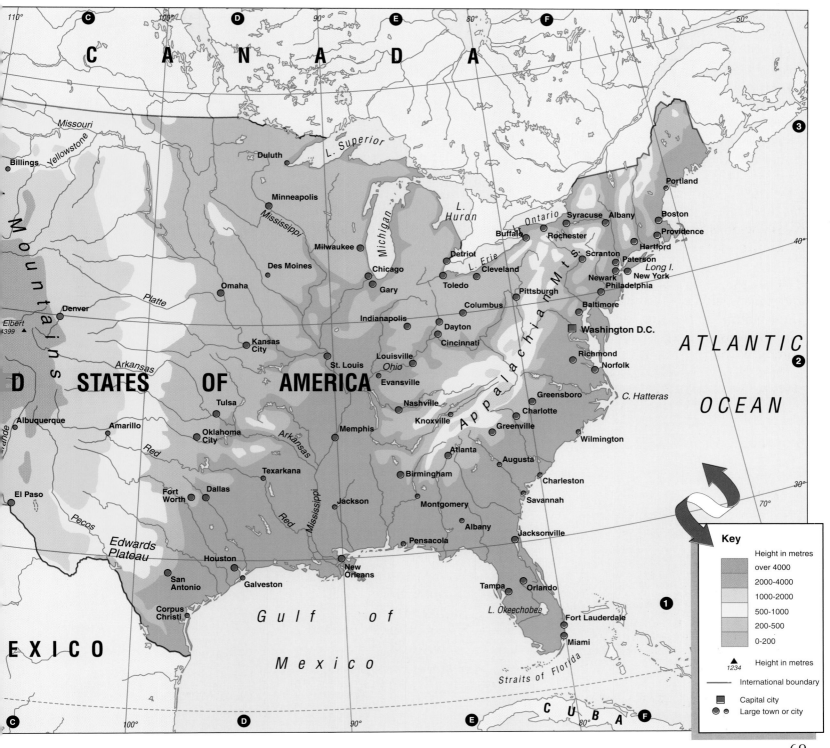

CANADA

UNITED STATES OF AMERICA

Missouri
Yellowstone
Billings
Duluth
L. Superior
Minneapolis
Mississippi
Milwaukee
L. Huron
L. Michigan
L. Ontario
Buffalo
Syracuse
Albany
Boston
Providence
Rochester
Hartford
Detriot
Scranton
Paterson
L. Erie
Cleveland
Long I.
Newark
New York
Des Moines
Chicago
Gary
Toledo
Pittsburgh
Philadelphia
Omaha
Columbus
Baltimore
Platte
Indianapolis
Dayton
Washington D.C.
Denver
Cincinnati
Elbert
4399
Kansas City
Louisville
Ohio
Richmond
Norfolk
Arkansas
St. Louis
Evansville
C. Hatteras
Tulsa
Nashville
Greensboro
Albuquerque
Knoxville
Charlotte
Amarillo
Oklahoma City
Memphis
Greenville
Red
Arkansas
Wilmington
Texarkana
Atlanta
Augusta
Fort Worth
Dallas
Birmingham
Charleston
Red
Mississippi
Jackson
Montgomery
Savannah
El Paso
Pecos
Albany
Jacksonville
Edwards Plateau
Pensacola
Houston
New Orleans
San Antonio
Galveston
Tampa
Orlando
Corpus Christi
L. Okeechobee
Fort Lauderdale
Gulf of Mexico
Miami
Straits of Florida
MEXICO
CUBA
ATLANTIC OCEAN
Rocky Mountains
Rio Grande
Appalachian Mts.

Key

Height in metres
over 4000
2000-4000
1000-2000
500-1000
200-500
0-200

▲ 1234 Height in metres
International boundary
■ Capital city
●● Large town or city

69

Canada, Greenland

Canada is a huge country which covers almost the whole of the northern part of North America. By land size Canada is the second largest country in the world.

East of Hudson Bay some of the world's most ancient rocks are to be found. This area is called the Canadian Shield. Rocks in the Shield have been dated to 4000 million years ago, and must have been formed not long after the earth itself came into being. South of Hudson Bay lie the Great Lakes, which form part of the border with the USA.

West of Hudson Bay the landscape of Canada is not so ancient. In the west lie the snow-capped peaks of the Rocky Mountains.

Between the Great Lakes and Rockies lies the Prairie. Prairie is an Indian name for the flat grasslands which extend for a thousand miles across southern Canada. Today the fertile soils of the prairie are used for farming.

The coastline of Nova Scotia is famous for its rugged scenery, sandy beaches and small fishing villages. ▼

▲ *The Rocky Mountains form the back-bone of the North American continent. People visit the mountains to enjoy the dramatic scenery and clear air.*

Farming is only possible in southern Canada. Towards the north the climate becomes too cold and harsh. A great belt of coniferous forest, of pine and other evergreen trees, covers the middle section of the country. North of the forest is the tundra, where the climate is too cold for trees, and only grasses and plants like moss and lichen can survive the long freezing winters.

Despite its huge land size Canada does not have a large population. Most people live and work in the south east, and particularly in the towns and cities around the Great Lakes and St Lawrence river.

Divided from Canada by Baffin Bay is Greenland. On maps Greenland looks like one large island, but in fact it is made up of several large islands, over which is spread the permanent Greenland ice cap. It would be difficult to think of a more unsuitable name, for 'green' is what the island is not! Less than one fifth of Greenland is free of the ice cap, and here very few plants grow.

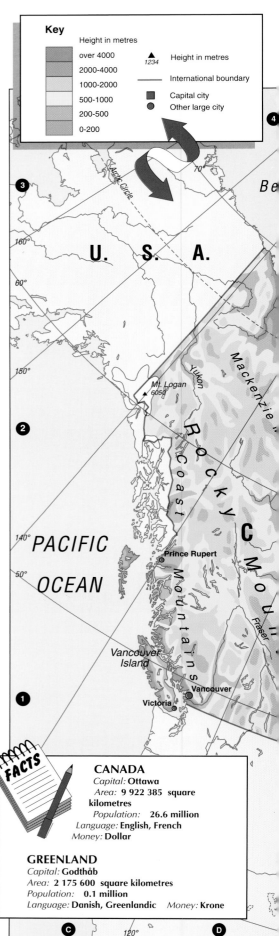

Key

Height in metres

	over 4000
	2000-4000
	1000-2000
	500-1000
	200-500
	0-200

▲ 1234 Height in metres

— International boundary

■ Capital city

● Other large city

U. S. A.

PACIFIC OCEAN

Mt. Logan 6050

Yukon

Mackenzie

Rocky Mountains

Coast Mountains

Fraser

Prince Rupert

Vancouver Island

Vancouver

Victoria

FACTS

CANADA
Capital: **Ottawa**
   Area: **9 922 385 square kilometres**
   Population: **26.6 million**
Language: **English, French**
Money: **Dollar**

GREENLAND
Capital: **Godthåb**
Area: **2 175 600 square kilometres**
Population: **0.1 million**
Language: **Danish, Greenlandic**   *Money:* **Krone**

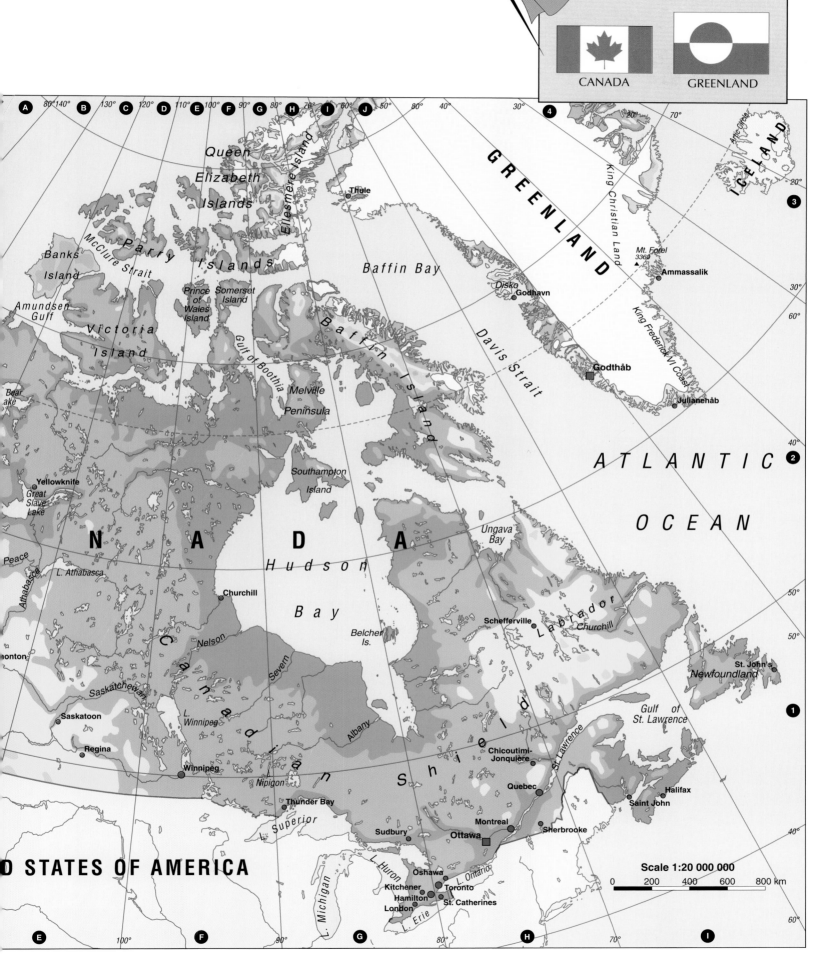

CANADA   GREENLAND

A 80°140° **B** 130° **C** 120° **D** 110° **E** 100° **F** 90° **G** 80° **H** 70° **I** 60° **J** 50° 40° 30° 20° 70° Artic Circle

G R E E N L A N D

I C E L A N D

Thule

Queen
Elizabeth
Islands

Ellesmere Island

King Christian Land

20°

4

3

Banks
Island

McClure Strait

Parry Islands

Baffin Bay

Disko
Godhavn

Mt. Forel
3360

Ammassalik

30°

Amundsen Gulf

Prince
of
Wales
Island

Somerset
Island

Baffin Island

King Frederick VI Coast

60°

Victoria Island

Gulf of Boothia

Melville
Peninsula

Davis Strait

Godthåb

40°

Bear
ake

A T L A N T I C

Julianehåb

Yellowknife

Great Slave Lake

Southampton
Island

O C E A N

N   **A**   **D**   **A**

40°

2

Peace

L. Athabasca

H u d s o n

Ungava
Bay

Athabasca

Churchill

Bay

Belcher
Is.

Schefferville

Labrador

Churchill

50°

50°

Saskatoon

Canadian

Nelson

Severn

St. John's
Newfoundland

Regina

L. Winnipeg

Albany

Shield

Chicoutimi-
Jonquière

Gulf of
St. Lawrence

1

Winnipeg

Nipigon

Quebec

St. Lawrence

Halifax

Saint John

Thunder Bay

Montreal

Sherbrooke

monton

L. Superior

Sudbury

Ottawa

D STATES OF AMERICA

L. Michigan

L. Huron

Oshawa

Kitchener

Hamilton

London

Toronto

St. Catherines

L. Ontario

L. Erie

40°

Scale 1:20 000 000

0   200   400   600   800 km

60°

E 100° **F** 90° **G** 80° **H** 70° **I**

71

Mexico, Guatemala, El Salvador, Belize

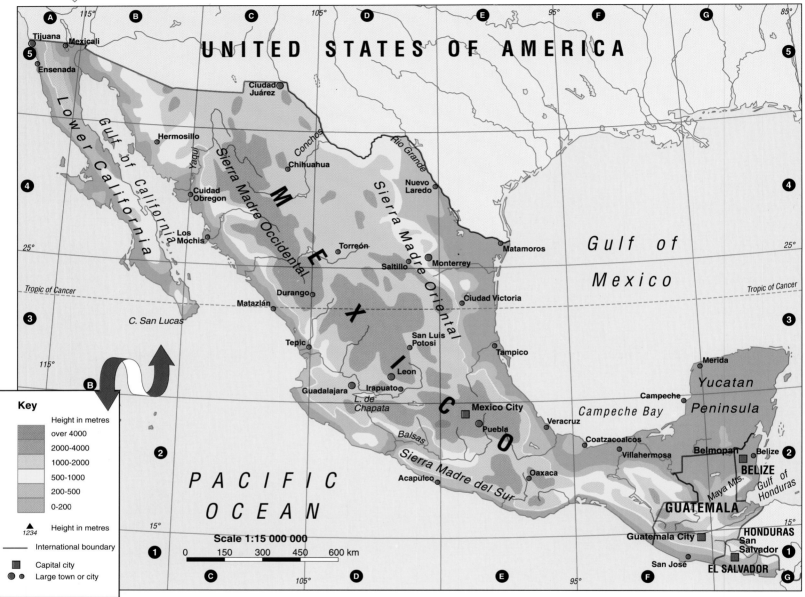

UNITED STATES OF AMERICA

Tijuana
Mexicali
Ensenada
Ciudad Juárez
Hermosillo
Chihuahua
Cuidad Obregon
Los Mochis
Torreón
Saltillo
Monterrey
Nuevo Laredo
Matamoros
Durango
Ciudad Victoria
Matazlán
C. San Lucas
Tepic
San Luis Potosi
Tampico
Leon
Guadalajara
Irapuato
L. de Chapata
Mexico City
Puebla
Veracruz
Merida
Coatzacoalcos
Villahermosa
Belmopan
Belize
Acapulco
Oaxaca
Guatemala City
San José
San Salvador

Lower California
Gulf of California
Sierra Madre Occidental
Sierra Madre Oriental
Sierra Madre del Sur
MEXICO
Balsas
Yucatan Peninsula
Campeche Bay
Gulf of Mexico
PACIFIC OCEAN
Maya Mts.
Gulf of Honduras
BELIZE
GUATEMALA
HONDURAS
EL SALVADOR

Tropic of Cancer

Key

Height in metres
- over 4000
- 2000-4000
- 1000-2000
- 500-1000
- 200-500
- 0-200

▲ 1234 Height in metres

— International boundary

■ Capital city

● ● Large town or city

Scale 1:15 000 000

0   150   300   450   600 km

Central America is the narrow strip of land between the two continents of North and South America. It is bordered to the west by the Pacific Ocean, and to the east by the Gulf of Mexico.

The language of most of Central America is Spanish. This is because the whole region was conquered by Spanish adventurers in 1519. These conquistadores, led by Hernando Cortes, overthrew the empire of the Aztecs when they captured the Aztec island city of Tenochtitlan.

By far the largest country in this region is Mexico. In such a large country as Mexico there are many different landscapes. In the north is the dry land of the Mexican desert. Most of the centre of the country is higher land, with snow-capped volcanoes, such as Popocatepetl. Some of the volcanoes are still active, and earthquakes also occur in this region. Even so this is the most densely populated part of Mexico. To the south east, in Yucatan, the land is covered in tropical forest.

BELIZE

EL SALVADOR

GUATEMALA

MEXICO

At present over 85 million people live in Mexico, but the number is growing rapidly. It has one of the fastest growing populations of any country in the world. This means that young people easily outnumber older people. Three quarters of all Mexicans are under the age of 30.

Almost half of all Mexican familes depend on farming for their living. Many of the farmers are very poor. The wealth of the country comes mainly from the oil and natural gas which was discovered in the 1970s. Oil and gas are exported to the USA.

The other countries are much smaller than Mexico. Belize has the smallest population, only 150 000 people, and is very different from neighbouring countries. The language spoken is English, as Belize was a British colony until 1981. In much of Central America the forest has been cleared to make more farmland, but in Belize much of the country is still tropical rain forest. Many types of animals and plants are thus being preserved in the forests of Belize.

MAYAN CIVILISATION

The ancient Mayan civilisation of Yucatan, Belize and Guatemala is famous for its great achievements in painting, astronomy and building. The Mayan civilisation began around 2000 BC, reaching it's peak between 250 AD and 900AD and lasted for nearly 3000 years .

Some of the buildings like the pyramid shaped temple at Chichén Itza in the photo above are still seen today by the growing numbers of tourists who visit the Yucatan. The map shows where some of the other famous buildings are found.

 FACTS

BELIZE
Capital: **Belmopan**
Area: **22 965 square kilometres**
Population: **0.2 million**
Language: **English** *Money:* **Dollar**

EL SALVADOR
Capital: **San Salvador**
Area: **21 395 square kilometres**
Population: **5.3 million**
Language: **Spanish** *Money:* **Colon**

GUATEMALA
Capital: **Guatemala City**
Area: **108 890 square kilometres**
Population: **9.2 million**
Language: **Spanish** *Money:* **Quetzal**

MEXICO
Capital: **Mexico City**
Area: **1 972 545 square kilometres**
Population: **86.2 million**
Language: **Spanish** *Money:* **Peso**

Mexico City, the capital of Mexico, was the capital of the Aztec Empire. It was conquered and rebuilt be the Spanish conquistadores in 1521. Fifty years ago, 1 million people lived in Mexico City. Today the number is around 20 million, and Mexico City is the largest city in the world. ▶

NORTH AMERICA

Bahamas, Cuba, Jamaica, Haiti, Dominican Republic, Puerto Rico, St Kitts-Nevis, Antigua and Barbuda, Dominica, St. Lucia, St Vincent, Grenada, Barbados, Trinidad and Tobago, Aruba, Netherland Antilles, Honduras, Nicaragua, Costa Rica, Panama

In the Caribbean Sea there are hundreds of islands. These islands form what are often called the West Indies. The West Indian islands stretch in a chain from the Bahamas just off the coast of Florida in North America, to Trinidad only a few miles off the coast of South America.

Few of the Indians who originally lived there survived the coming of European explorers and settlers. The warm, wet climate of the islands was good for growing crops such as sugar and spices, which could not be grown in Europe. To work the farms black people were brought from Africa as slaves. Today the people of the Caribbean are a mix of people whose ancestors came from Africa and Europe. All but a few islands are now independent countries.

Most of the people who live in the islands today earn their living from farming although tourists from America and Europe are an important source of money for many islands.

▲ *More than 15 000 ships pass through the Panama Canal each year. It now provides a 'Short-cut' between the Pacific and Atlantic Oceans.*

The narrowest point in Central America lies in the Isthmus of Panama. Here the distance between the Pacific and Atlantic Oceans is only 65km. In 1880 a French company began to dig a canal to join the two oceans but it was only completed in 1914 by the United States. The canal saves ships having to sail thousands of extra miles around Cape Horn at the southern tip of South America.

Country	Capital	Area (Sq. Km's)	Population	Language	Money
ANTIGUA & BARBUDA	St. John's	442	0.08 million	English	EC Dollar
ARUBA	Oranjestad	193	0.06 million	Dutch, Papiamento	A Floria
BAHAMAS	Nassau	13 865	0.3 million	English	Dollar
BARBADOS	Bridgetown	430	0.25 million	English	Dollar
COSTA RICA	San Jose	50 900	3.0 million	Spanish	Colón
CUBA	Havana	114 525	10.6 million	Spanish	Peso
DOMINICA	Roseau	751	0.08 million	English, French	EC Dollar
DOMINICAN REPUBLIC	Santo Domingo	48 440	7.2 million	Spanish	Peso
GRENADA	St. George's	345	0.08 million	English	EC Dollar
HAITI	Port-au-Prince	27 750	6.5 million	French, Creole	Gourde
HONDURAS	Tegucigalpa	112 085	5.1 million	Spanish	Lempira
JAMAICA	Kingston	11 425	2.4 million	English	Dollar
NETHERLAND ANTILLES	Willemstad	800	0.18 million	Dutch, English Papiamento	NA Guilder
NICARAGUA	Managua	148 000	3.9 million	Spanish	Cordoba
PANAMA	Panama City	78 515	2.4 million	Spanish	Balboa
PUERTO RICO	San Juan	8 897	3.6 million	Spanish, English	US Dollar
ST KITTS-NEVIS	Basseterre	261	0.04 million	English	EC Dollar
ST. LUCIA	Castries	616	0.15 million	English	EC Dollar
ST. VINCENT	Kingstown	389	0.12 million	English	EC Dollar
TRINIDAD AND TOBAGO	Port of Spain	5 130	1.2 million	English	Dollar

Key

Height in metres
- over 4000
- 2000-4000
- 1000-2000
- 500-1000
- 200-500
- 0-200

▲ 1234 — Height in metres

——— International boundary

■ Capital city

◉ Large town or city

ANTIGUA & BARBUDA · ARUBA · BAHAMAS · BARBADOS

COSTA RICA · CUBA · DOMINICA · DOMINICAN REPUBLIC

GRENADA · HAITI · HONDURAS · JAMAICA

U.S.A.

Freeport
Grand Bahama
Great Abaco I.

80°   75°

25°

Andros I.   Nassau

Tropic of Cancer

70°   Turks and Caicos Is. (U.K.)

65°   60°

Scale 1:10 500 000

0   100   200   300   400 km

Santa Clara

Camagüey

Holguín

Bayamo

Santiago de Cuba   Guantánamo

Puerto Plata
Santiago
La Vega

HAITI
Port-au-Prince   DOMINICAN REP.

Santo Domingo

Arecibo   San Juan
Carolina
Mayaguez   Caguas
Ponce   PUERTO RICO

British Virgin Is. (U.K.)

Anguilla (U.K.)

Virgin Is. (U.S.A.)

NETH. ANTILLES
ST. KITTS-NEVIS

ANTIGUA AND BARBUDA
St John's

Leeward Islands

Montego Bay

JAMAICA   Kingston

Greater Antilles

Hispaniola

Guadeloupe (Fr.)
Basse Terre

DOMINICA
Rosseau

Islands

Caribbean

Sea

Lesser   Antilles

Martinique (Fr.)
Fort-de-France

Castries
ST. LUCIA
Kingstown
ST. VINCENT AND THE GRENADINES

Bridgetown
BARBADOS

St. George's
GRENADA

Windward Islands

ARUBA
Oranjestad

NETHERLANDS ANTILLES

Willemstad

TRINIDAD & TOBAGO

Port of Spain

70°   65°   10°

Colon
San Miguelito
PANAMA
Panama City

Gulf of Darien

Gulf of Panama

COLOMBIA

80°   75°

NETHERLAND ANTILLES · NICARAGUA · PANAMA · PUERTO RICO

ST. KITTS - NEVIS · ST. LUCIA · ST. VINCENT · TRINIDAD & TOBAGO

75

Countries

ATLANTIC OCEAN

CENTRAL AMERICA

Caribbean Sea

Barranquilla
Maracaibo Caracas
TRINIDAD AND TOBAGO

VENEZUELA

Georgetown
Paramaribo
Medellín
Bogotá
GUYANA SURINAM Cayenne
COLOMBIA
FRENCH GUIANA
(France)
Cali

Galapagos Islands
(Ecuador)

Equator   Equator

Quito
ECUADOR
Guayaquil
Belém
Manaus

Fortaleza

PERU

Trujillo

B R A Z I L

Recife

Lima

Salvador

La Paz
Brasília

B O L I V I A
Sucre

PARAGUAY

São Paulo   Rio de Janeiro
Asunción
Curitiba

PACIFIC

OCEAN

Córdoba
Mendoza
Rosario

Pôrto Alegre

ATLANTIC

OCEAN

Santiago

CHILE

ARGENTINA

Buenos
Aires
URUGUAY
Montevideo

Tropic of Capricorn   Tropic of Capricorn

Falkland Islands
(U.K.)

Key
— International boundary
■ Capital city
● Other large city

Scale 1 : 40 000 000
0   400   800   1200   1600 km

South Georgia
(U.K.)

CENTRAL AMERICA

Caribbean Sea

Cape Gallinas

Trinidad

Orinoco

Guiana Highlands

Cordillera Occidental
Cordillera Central
Cordillera Oriental

Galapagos Islands   Equator

Negro

Amazon

Mt. Chimborazo
▲ 6272

Amazon

Madeira

Tapajos

Tocantins

Cape São Roque

Cape Negra

S e l v a s

A N D E S

PACIFIC OCEAN

L. Titicaca

Atacama

L. Poopo

Mato Grosso Upland

São Francisco

East Brazilian Highlands

Desert

Gran Chaco

Paraguay

Tropic of Capricorn

Cape Frio

Tropic of Capricorn

ATLANTIC OCEAN

Key

Height in metres

over 4000
2000-4000
1000-2000
500-1000
200-500
0-200

Land covered by ice

▲
1234   Height in metres

Mt. Aconcagua
▲ 6960

Paraná

Uruguay

Rio de la Plata

A N D E S

Pampas

Patagonia

Scale 1 : 40 000 000

0   400   800   1200   1600 km

Falkland Islands

Tierra del Fuego

Magellan's Strait

Cape Horn

South Georgia

ATLANTIC OCEAN

ATLANTIC OCEAN

Equator

Colombia, Venezuela, Guyana, Surinam, French Guiana, Ecuador, Peru, Bolivia

In Ecuador is Cotopaxi, which at 5897 metres is the world's highest active volcano.

The western side of South America is dominated by the Andes mountains, which run from north to south through the whole continent. Many of the mountains in the Andes are volcanoes, such as Huascaran in Peru and Cotopaxi in Ecuador. This region is one of the most active places on the earth's crust. The Andes mountains are still slowly rising. There are frequent earthquakes as well as volcanic eruptions. East of the Andes the land slopes down to the Amazon river basin.

Much of this region was once part of the empire of the Inca People. The Inca Empire began to grow in about 1350 AD and in less than 200 years it extended for 3000 km along the Andes. The Inca capital was at Cuzco, in what is now Peru.

Spaniards settled most of this part of South America, and today Spanish is the main language. Descendants of the original Indian peoples still speak a language called Quechua. The Spanish brought their religion too, and now the majority of people are Roman Catholics.

In the north of the region is Venezuela, which is a wealthy country by South American standards. The wealth is based on the oil which is taken from under the water of Lake Maracaibo. Colombia is the world's second largest exporter of coffee, which is grown in the foothills of the Andes. In recent years Colombia has become the centre of the drugs trade, and huge amounts of illegal drugs are produced and smuggled into countries such as the USA.

Peru is the largest country in the region. Most people live on the lower land near the coast, where the capital city of Lima is located. However, people still live and farm high in the mountains in a region called the altiplano. This plain, between two snow-capped ridges of the Andes, has some of the highest farmland on earth. Farmers grow potatoes, and herd animals such as llama and alpaca.

Bolivia, the most southerly country in this region, is landlocked and has no coast. Much of the country is at a high altitude.

La Paz, situated in the Andes in Bolivia, is the highest capital city in the world. The name 'La Paz' means peace. ▼

FACTS

BOLIVIA
Capital: **La Paz**
Area: **1 098 575 square kilometres**
Population: **7.4 million**
Language: **Spanish**
Money: **Boliviano**

COLOMBIA
Capital: **Bogota**
Area: **1 138 915 square kilometres**
Population: **33.0 million**
Language: **Spanish**
Money: **Peso**

ECUADOR
Capital: **Quito**
Area: **461 475 square kilometres**
Population: **10.8 million**
Language: **Spanish**
Money: **Sucre**

FRENCH GUIANA
Capital: **Cayenne**
Area: **91 000 square kilometres**
Population: **0.1 million**
Language: **French**
Money: **French Franc**

GUYANA
Capital: **Georgetown**
Area: **214 970 square kilometres**
Population: **0.8 million**
Language: **English**
Money: **Dollar**

PERU
Capital: **Lima**
Area: **1 285 215 square kilometres**
Population: **21.6 million**
Language: **Spanish, Quechua**
Money: **Sol**

SURINAM
Capital: **Paramaribo**
Area: **163 820 square kilometres**
Population: **0.4 million**
Language: **Dutch, English**
Money: **Guilder**

VENEZUELA
Capital: **Caracas**
Area: **912 045 square kilometres**
Population: **19.7 million**
Language: **Spanish**
Money: **Bolivar**

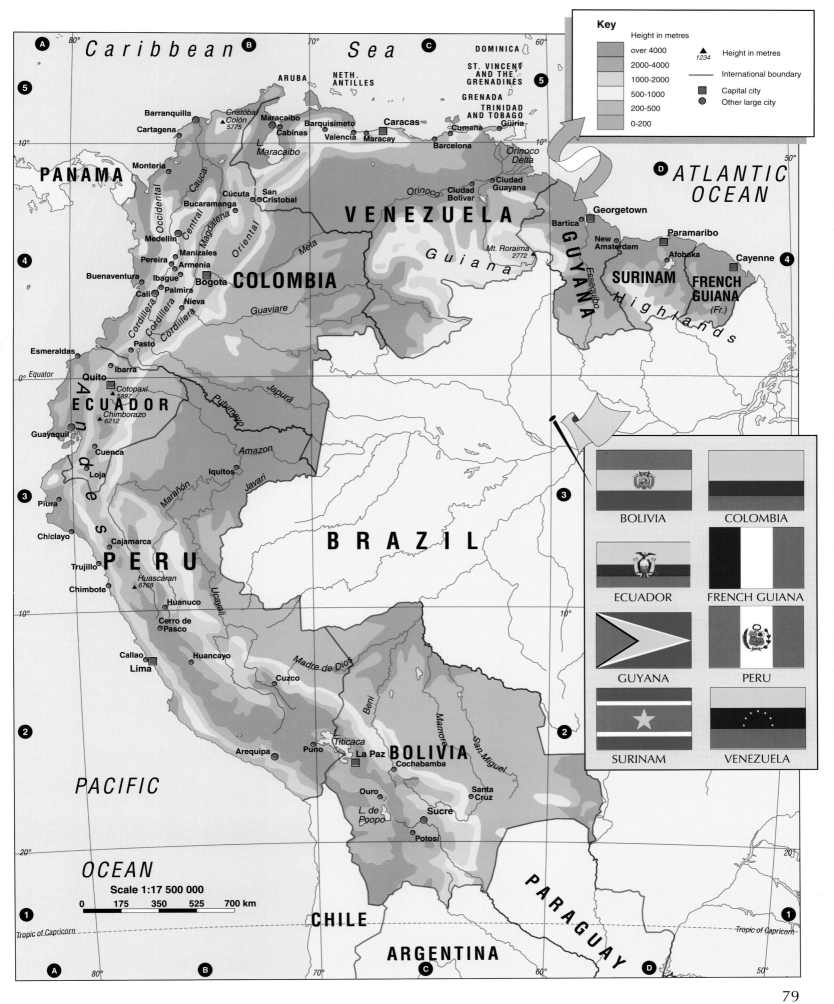

Key

Height in metres

over 4000
2000-4000
1000-2000
500-1000
200-500
0-200

▲ 1234 Height in metres

— International boundary

■ Capital city

● Other large city

Caribbean

A · 80° B · 70° C · 60° Sea DOMINICA

ARUBA
NETH. ANTILLES

ST. VINCENT AND THE GRENADINES

GRENADA
TRINIDAD AND TOBAGO

Barranquilla
Cartagena
Cristóbal Colón 5775 ▲
Maracaibo
Cabinas
Barquisimeto
Valencia
Maracay
Caracas
Cumaná
Güiria
Barcelona
L. Maracaibo

10°

D ATLANTIC OCEAN

50°

PANAMA

Monteria
Cúcuta
San Cristobal
Bucaramanga

COLOMBIA

Medellin
Manizales
Pereira
Armenia
Ibague
Buenaventura
Cali
Palmira
Bogota
Nieva
Pasto

Occidental
Cauca
Central
Magdalena
Oriental
Cordillera
Cordillera
Cordillera

VENEZUELA

Orinoco
Meta
Guaviare
Ciudad Bolivar
Ciudad Guayana
Orinoco Delta

Guiana

Mt. Roraima 2772

Bartica
Georgetown
New Amsterdam
Afobaka
Paramaribo
Cayenne

GUYANA
SURINAM
FRENCH GUIANA (Fr.)

Essequibo
Highlands

Esmeraldas
Ibarra
Quito
Cotopaxi 5897 ▲

0° Equator

ECUADOR
Chimborazo 6212 ▲

Guayaquil
Cuenca
Loja

A
n
d
e
s

Putumayo
Japurá
Amazon
Iquitos
Javari
Marañón
Ucayali

BRAZIL

Piura

3

Chiclayo
Cajamarca
Trujillo

PERU

Huascaran 6768 ▲
Chimbote
Huanuco
Cerro de Pasco

Madre de Dios
Beni
Mamore
San Miguel

Callao
Lima
Huancayo
Cuzco

Arequipa
Puno
L. Titicaca
La Paz
Cochabamba

BOLIVIA

PACIFIC

Ouro
Santa Cruz
Sucre

L. de Poopo

OCEAN

Potosi

20°

Scale 1:17 500 000

0   175   350   525   700 km

1

Tropic of Capricorn

CHILE

PARAGUAY

Tropic of Capricorn

ARGENTINA

A · 80° B · 70° C · 60° D · 50°

BOLIVIA	COLOMBIA
ECUADOR	FRENCH GUIANA
GUYANA	PERU
SURINAM	VENEZUELA

79

Brazil

Almost half of the whole continent of South America is taken up by one country - Brazil. It is the fifth largest country in the world. The whole of the northern part of Brazil is covered by the tropical rainforest of the Amazon Basin. This is the largest area of tropical forest on earth. This region lies on the Equator, and the climate is hot and wet throughout the year. The heat and moisture allow a great number of types, or species, of plants and animals to thrive in the thick forest. 55 000 species of flowering plants are found in Brazil, and over half of them exist only in the Amazon forests.

The Brazilians have tried to develop the Amazon region in different ways. Because the forest is so huge, and difficult for travel, the government has built some roads across the region. This has allowed people to clear the land, either for farming or for the valuable hardwood of the great trees. Large parts of the forest are cleared each year, and many people now believe this to be a serious problem. When the forest is cleared the soils very quickly lose their fertility, and the land has to be abandoned. Around 1 percent of the total area of forest is lost each year.

▲ As well as being a port, Rio de Janeiro is famous for its magnificent setting. Many tourists visit Sugar Loaf Mountain and Copacabana Beach.

Much of Brazil's population, and most of its industries, are located in the south east. It is here that two of the world's top ten largest cities are found - São Paulo and Rio de Janeiro. Amongst the millions of people who live in the cities, there are great differences in wealth. Wealthy Brazilians contrast with the poorer people who live in makeshift shanty towns - or favelas - around the edge of the cities.

FACTS

BRAZIL
Capital: **Brasilia**
Area: **8 511 965 square kilometres**
Population: **150.4 million**
Language: **Portuguese**
Money: **Cruzeiro**

AMAZON RAINFOREST

Macapá
Belém
Manaus · Amazon
Santárem
São Luís
Trans Amazonian Highway
Pôrto Velho

B r a z i l

· Brasilia

■ Tropical rainforest
☐ Other Vegetation
▨ Areas where over 50% of the rainforest has been lost
— Main roads
- - Roads under construction
— Extent of Amazon Region

Rio de Janeiro
São Paulo ·

BRAZIL

GUYANA

Boa Vista

Branco

Negro

Madeira

Roosevelt

Tapajós

Xingu

Araguaia

Tocantins

Guaporé

Pôrto
Velho

v   a   s

B   R   A   Z   I   L

Planalto   do
Mato   Grosso

Mato Grosso

Cuiabá

LIVIA

Manaus

Santarem

Amazon

Amazon
Delta

Marajó I.

Macapá

Belém

São Luís

Santarem

Sobral   Fortaleza

Teresina

Parnaiba

Mossoró

C. São Roque

Natal

Campina Grande   João Pessoa

Caruaru   Recife

Maceió

Aracaju

Brazilian

São Francisco

Feira de
Santana

Salvador

Vitoria da
Conquista   Itabuna

Brasília

Goiânia   Highlands Montes Claros

Tres Marias
Dam

Uberlândia

Uberaba

Governador
Valadares

Belo Horizonte

Scale 1:17 500 000

0   175   350   525   700 km

Campo
Grande

São José
do Rio Prêto

Ribeirâo
Prêto

Bauru

Volta
Redonda

Petrópolis
Niterói

Campos

Vitória

Campinas

Londrina   Sorocaba   Jundiaí

São Paulo   Rio de Janeiro

Paraná

PARAGUAY

GENTINA

Santos

Ponta Grossa   Curitiba

Tropic of Capricorn

Florianópolis

Santa
María   Canôas

Pôrto Alegre

L. Patos

Pelotas

Uruguay

Rio Grande

URUGUAY

Equator   0°

10°

20°

30°

50°   40°   30°

60°

Key

Height in metres

over 4000

2000-4000

1000-2000

500-1000

200-500

0-200

Height in metres
1234

International boundary

Capital city

Large town or city

81

Chile, Argentina, Paraguay, Uruguay

The largest country in this region is Argentina. On the western border of the country are the Andes, rising to their highest point in the continent at the extinct volcano of Aconcagua (6960m). East of the mountains lie the pampas, a huge, almost flat grassland plain. The word 'pampas' in the local Indian language means 'flat, featureless plain'. The soil here is very fertile, and the grasslands have been taken over for farming. In the past - and in some places still today - the cattle were herded by the gauchos, or Argentinean cowboys. Today there are 60 million cattle and 35 million sheep in Argentina.

Most of the people in the country live in the cities, and particularly in the capital city, Buenos Aires, which has a population of over 10 million.

Between the two largest countries in South America - Argentina and Brazil - lies the smaller country of Uruguay. As in its neighbour Argentina, most Uruguayans are the descendants of families who migrated from southern Europe. By far the largest city is the capital, Montevideo.

Gauchos, or cowboys, herd sheep and cattle on the pampas. Argentina is the world's third largest exporter of wool and the third largest producer of beef.

Chile is dominated by the Andes mountains. The southern Andes are very cold and snowy. The scenery in this part of Chile is bleak, and very few people live here.

ARGENTINA
Capital: **Buenos Aires**
Area: **2 777 815 square kilometres**
Population: **32.3 million**
Language: **Spanish**
Money: **Austral**

CHILE
Capital: **Santiago**
Area: **751 625 square kilometres**
Population: **13.2 million**
Language: **Spanish**   *Money:* **Peso**

PARAGUAY
Capital: **Asuncion**
Area: **406 750 square kilometres**
Population: **4.3 million**
Language: **Spanish, Guarani** *Money:* **Guarani**

URUGUAY
Capital: **Montevideo**
Area: **186 925 square kilometres**
Population: **3.1 million**
Language: **Spanish**   *Money:* **Uruguayan Peso**

CROSS SECTION OF SOUTH AMERICA

The diagram below extends from Chile in the west to Argentina and Uruguay in the east and shows the land use.

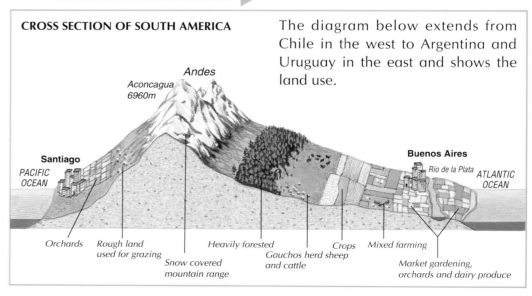

Andes
Aconcagua 6960m
Santiago
PACIFIC OCEAN
Buenos Aires
Rio de la Plata   ATLANTIC OCEAN

Orchards   Rough land used for grazing   Snow covered mountain range   Heavily forested   Gauchos herd sheep and cattle   Crops   Mixed farming   Market gardening, orchards and dairy produce

PERU

BOLIVIA

BRAZIL

Atacama Desert

Arica
Iquique
Antofagasta

PACIFIC

OCEAN

Coquimbo

Aconcagua
6960

Viña del Mar
Valparaíso
Santiago
Rancagua

Talcahuano
Concepción

Temuco

Valdivia

Puerto Montt

Chiloé I.

San Valentín
4058

Murallón
3600

Bahía
Grande

Magellans Str.

Punta Arenas

Cape Horn

Tierra del
Fuego

Salta

San Miguel
de Tucumán

Santiago del
Estero

SanJuan

Mendoza

Córdoba

Talca

Chillán

ARGENTINA

Colorado

Salado

Negro

G. of San Matias

G. of San Jorge

Gran Chaco

Pilcomayo

Bermejo

Salado

Paraná

Pampas

Patagonia

Concepción

PARAGUAY
Asunción
Villarica

Corrientes

Entre Rios

Paraguay

Uruguay

Santa Fé
Paraná

Rosario

URUGUAY

Negro

Buenos
Aires

La
Plata

Montevideo

Rio de la
Plata

Mar del Plata

Bahía
Blanca

Bahía
Blanca

SOUTH
ATLANTIC
OCEAN

Scale 1:17 500 000

0   175   350   525   700 km

Falkland Is. (U.K.)

Stanley

Tropic of Capricorn

Flags:
ARGENTINA   CHILE
PARAGUAY   URUGUAY

Sharing a border with Argentina is Chile. In the north of Chile is the Atacama desert, one of the driest places on earth. In some places in the Atacama no rain has been recorded in living memory. In contrast, southern Chile extends into the almost uninhabited region of Patagonia and Tierra del Fuego, with its coastal fjords, icebergs and bitter winters.

The other country in this region is Paraguay. Unlike the other countries in the region, three quarters of all Paraguayans are the descendants of the Indian peoples who lived in South America before Europeans arrived. However, much of the land in Paraguay is owned by a few hundred families of European descent.

Off the coast of Argentina lie the Falkland Islands, or the Islas Malvinas as they are called by Argentineans.

These very European-looking houses are actually in the Falkland Islands, in the South Atlantic Ocean. The islands are a colony of the UK, although Argentina would like to claim them.

Key

Height in metres
over 4000
2000-4000
1000-2000
500-1000
200-500
0-200

▲   Height in metres
1234

────   International boundary

■   Capital city

● ∘   Large town or city

Micronesia, Marshall Islands, Nauru, Solomon Islands, Tuvalu, Kiribati, Cook Islands, French Polynesia

The Pacific is the largest and deepest ocean in the world. Almost half of the world's water is found in the Pacific.

The islands of the Pacific can be divided into three groups. In the central Pacific lie the islands of Polynesia. Most, like Tahiti, are volcanic islands. Polynesian islanders are superb navigators. For centuries they have been sailing their canoes over huge areas of the Pacific.

In the west lie the islands of Melanesia. Many different cultures and languages are found in Melanesia. On some isolated islands a language may be spoken by only a few hundred people. In the southwest are two thousand or so islands of Micronesia, many of them coral atolls.

Most of the Pacific countries consist of many scattered islands. Kiribati, for example, has around 28 islands.

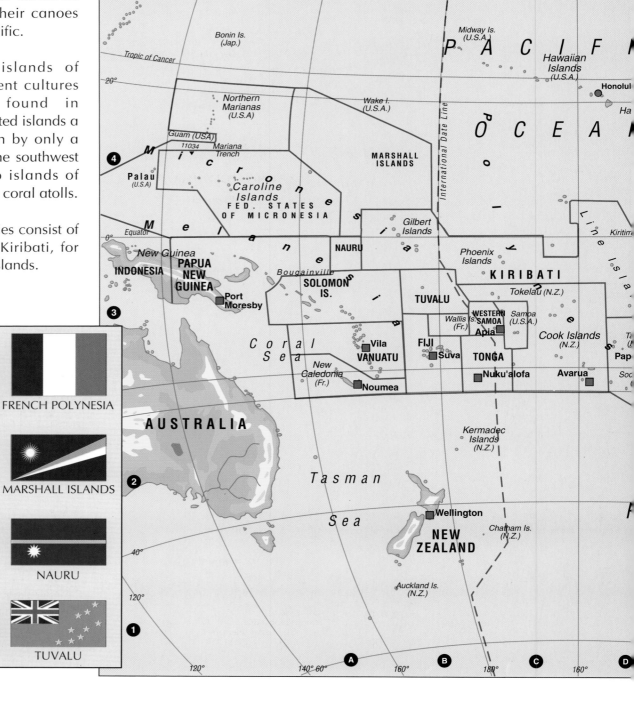

COOK ISLANDS

FRENCH POLYNESIA

KIRIBATI

MARSHALL ISLANDS

MICRONESIA

NAURU

SOLOMON ISLANDS

TUVALU

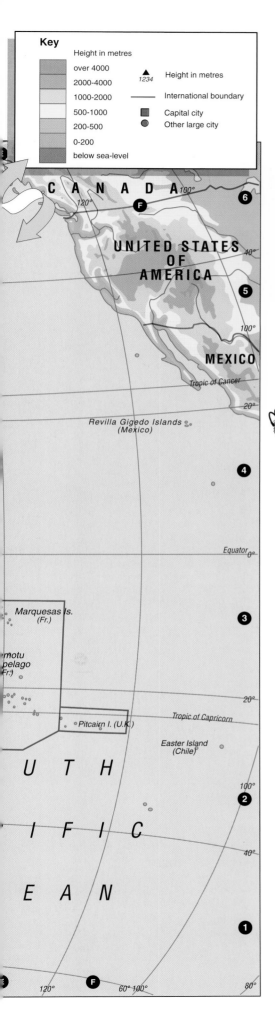

Key

Height in metres

over 4000
2000-4000
1000-2000
500-1000
200-500
0-200

below sea-level

▲ Height in metres
1234

International boundary

Capital city

Other large city

CANADA

UNITED STATES OF AMERICA

MEXICO

Tropic of Cancer

Revilla Gigedo Islands (Mexico)

Equator

Marquesas Is. (Fr.)

motu pelago (Fr.)

Tropic of Capricorn

Pitcairn I. (U.K.)

Easter Island (Chile)

SOUTH PACIFIC OCEAN

The islands of Hawaii which were discovered by Captain Cook in 1778, became a state of the USA in 1959. Hawaii consists of more than 20 volcanic islands and atolls. The beautiful beaches and warm sunny climate are very popular with holiday-makers.

FACTS

COOK ISLANDS
Capital: **Avarua**
Area: **293 square kilometres**
Population: **18 thousand**
Language: **English, Maori**
Money: **Dollar**

FRENCH POLYNESIA
Capital: **Papeete**
Area: **3 265 square kilometres**
Population: **206 thousand**
Language: **French, Tahitian**
Money: **Pacific Franc**

KIRIBATI
Capital: **Bairiki on Tarawa**
Area: **684 square kilometres**
Population: **66 thousand**
Language: **English**
Money: **Australian Dollar**

MICRONESIA
Capital: **Palikir on Pohnpei**
Area: **702 square kilometres**
Population: **99 thousand**
Language: **English**
Money: **Dollar**

MARSHALL ISLANDS
Capital: **Dalap-Uliga-Darrit**
Area: **181 square kilometres**
Population: **40 thousand**
Language: **English, Marshallese**
Money: **Dollar**

NAURU
Capital: **Yaren**
Area: **21 square kilometres**
Population: **10 thousand**
Language: **Nauruan, English**
Money: **Australian Dollar**

SOLOMON ISLANDS
Capital: **Honiara**
Area: **29 790 square kilometres**
Population: **321 thousand**
Language: **English**
Money: **Dollar**

TUVALU
Capital: **Fongafale**
Area: **25 square kilometres**
Population: **10 thousand**
Language: **English, Tuvaluan**
Money: **Dollar**

A very simple and traditional way of life is followed by many people on the Pacific islands. Living in small villages, people often survive on fruit and vegetables grown in gardens and fish caught from hand-carved canoes.

On some of the larger islands, people work on large plantations, where coconuts, sugar-cane and bananas are grown. More and more islands such as Fiji and Hawaii are attracting tourists who can afford the air-fares to these remote places.

One of the most remote of the Pacific islands is Easter Island. It was discovered on Easter Sunday in 1722 and has belonged to Chile since 1888. The island's most remarkable features are the gigantic stone sculptures. These were built and lifted completely by hand by the original aborigine inhabitants.

Australia, Papua New Guinea

AUSTRALIA   PAPUA NEW GUINEA

FACTS

AUSTRALIA
Capital: **Canberra**
Area: **7 682 300 square kilometres**
Population: **17.1 million**
Language: **English** *Money:* **Dollar**

PAPUA NEW GUINEA
Capital: **Port Moresby**
Area: **462 840 square kilometres**
Population: **3.7 million**
Language: **English** *Money:* **Kina**

Australia is the world's largest island. Although the country is huge it does not have a large population - just over 17 million. Much of the country is very dry, and most of the centre and west of Australia is desert. Only in the east is the climate suitable for many types of farming. Most of Australia's people live in cities around the coast.

The first people to inhabit Australia were the aborigines, who first arrived about 40 000 years ago. The aborigines were nomadic hunter gatherers - they did not settle in one place. Their way of life was ideally suited to the climate and landscape of the country. Many beautiful aboriginal cave paintings and rock carvings can be seen at their holy places, such as Uluru on the majestic Ayers Rock.

The first Europeans to reach Australia were Dutch sailors in the 1600s, who explored the north, west and south coasts. They found these areas too inhospitable for people to live, and so did not explore further. This changed when Captain James Cook discovered the fertile east coast in 1770. The first settlement was a prison colony set up at Botany Bay (near modern day Sydney) in 1778. As more people came to Australia, mainly from Britain, the land near the east coast began to be farmed. Sheep and cattle were raised and crops such as wheat and fruit were grown.

The first big increase in population came in the mid 1800s, when gold was discovered. The gold rush brought in prospectors, hoping to strike lucky and get rich. 'Gold towns' such as Bendigo in Victoria and Coolgardie in Western Australia sprang up almost overnight. The gold rush did not last, but people continued to come to Australia. Today's Australians had their family beginnings in many parts of Europe and the rest of the world.

The only large city in the west of Australia is Perth. It is so remote from the other main cities of the east coast , that to travel by train from Perth to Sydney takes three days and three nights.

▲ *Very few people live in the dry central plain of the Australian 'outback'. Many of those who do live here, work on huge sheep farms. Australia is by far the world's largest producer of wool.*

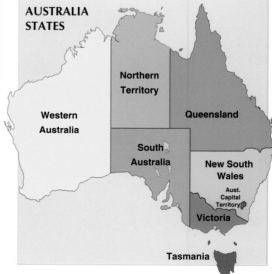

AUSTRALIA STATES

Northern Territory

Western Australia

Queensland

South Australia

New South Wales

Aust. Capital Territory

Victoria

Tasmania

Key

Height in metres

over 4000
2000-4000
1000-2000
500-1000
200-500
0-200
below sea-level

▲
1234 Height in metres

International boundary

Capital city

Large town or city

INDONESIA

Arafura Sea

Timor Sea

Bismarck Sea

PAPUA NEW
GUINEA

Sepik
Mt. Hagen
Wewak
Madang
Mt. Wilhelm 4694 ▲
Lae
New Britain

Torres Strait

C. Hope **Port Moresby**

Darwin C. Arnhem
Arnhem Land

Gulf of Carpentaria

C. Melville

Coral Sea

Wyndham

Mitchell

Cairns

Great Sandy Desert

Tennant Creek

Mount Isa

Flinders

Townsville

Port Hedland

Tropic of Capricorn

Hamersley Range
Mount Newman

Macdonnell Ranges
Alice Springs

Simpson Desert

Barcaldine

Great Dividing Range

Rockhampton
Gladstone

Gibson Desert

Gascoyne

Musgrave Ranges

A U S T R A L I A

Great Artesian Basin

Grey Range

Murchison

Great Victoria Desert

L. Eyre

Brisbane

Mount Magnet

Bourke

Geraldton

Darling

Kalgoorlie

Nullarbor Plain

Woomera

Cessnock
Newcastle

Eucla

Port Augusta

Lachlan

Bathurst

Sydney

Whyalla
Port Pirie

Perth
Northam

Murray

Wagga Wagga

Wollongong

Fremantle

Bunbury
Augusta

Esperance

Adelaide

Albury

Great Dividing Range

Canberra
Mt. Kosciusko 2230

Albany

Great

INDIAN

Mount Gambier

Melbourne

Geelong

Tasman Sea

Bass Strait

OCEAN

Devonport

Tasmania

Hobart

Scale 1:20 000 000

0   200   400   600   800 km

87

New Zealand, Fiji, Vanuatu, New Caledonia, Western Samoa, Tonga

In the South Pacific Ocean lies New Zealand, which is made up of two main islands - North Island and South Island. Much of New Zealand is mountainous. In the north there are volcanoes, and places where hot springs and geysers are found. The climate ranges from warm and tropical in the north, to the snow capped peaks and glaciers of the Southern Alps in the south.

The first settlers were the Maoris, who reached New Zealand after sailing across the Pacific from the islands of Polynesia. Later the country became a British colony, and people moved to New Zealand from Europe. Today farming is still the most important occupation, employing 10 percent of the population. New Zealand is one of the world's leading exporters of beef, mutton and wool.

FIJI
Capital: **Suva**
Area: **18 330 square kilometres**
Population: **0.8 million**
Language: **English, Fiji, Hindi**
Money: **Dollar**

NEW CALEDONIA
Capital: **Noumea**
Area: **19 058 square kilometres**
Population: **0.2 million**
Language: **French**   *Money:* **Pacific Franc**

NEW ZEALAND
Capital: **Wellington**
Area: **265 150 square kilometres**
Population: **3.3 million**
Language: **English, Maori**   *Money:* **Dollar**

TONGA
Capital: **Nuku'alofa**
Area: **699 square kilometres**
Population: **0.1 million**
Language: **English, Tongan**   *Money:* **Pa'anga**

VANUATU
Capital: **Vila**
Area: **14 765 square kilometres**
Population: **0.15 million**
Language: **English, French, Bislama**
Money: **Vatu**

WESTERN SAMOA
Capital: **Apia**
Area: **2 840 square kilometres**
Population: **0.16 million**
Language: **Samoan, English**   *Money:* **Tala**

In the Pacific there are thousands of islands. Some islands, such as New Zealand, are quite large, but most are small. Together these islands form what is called Oceania. Many of the islands are the tips of mountains or volcanoes which rise up from the ocean floor. Other islands are made of coral. Coral is formed from the hard shells of tiny sea creatures, called polyps. Over thousands of years the polyps die, and their shells become cemented together to form coral atolls and reefs.

In the volcanic areas of the North Island of New Zealand, natural underground hot steam is piped to power stations and used to make electricity. This is called 'geo-thermal' power.

Many of the smaller island groups in Oceania are covered with dense tropical vegetation. The high temperatures and heavy rainfall mean that the main crops produced are coconuts, bananas and rice. On some islands, such as Fiji, tourism is becoming more important.

In this traditional village in Fiji, the coconut palm trees provide the materials for house-building as well as coconuts for export.

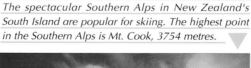

The spectacular Southern Alps in New Zealand's South Island are popular for skiing. The highest point in the Southern Alps is Mt. Cook, 3754 metres.

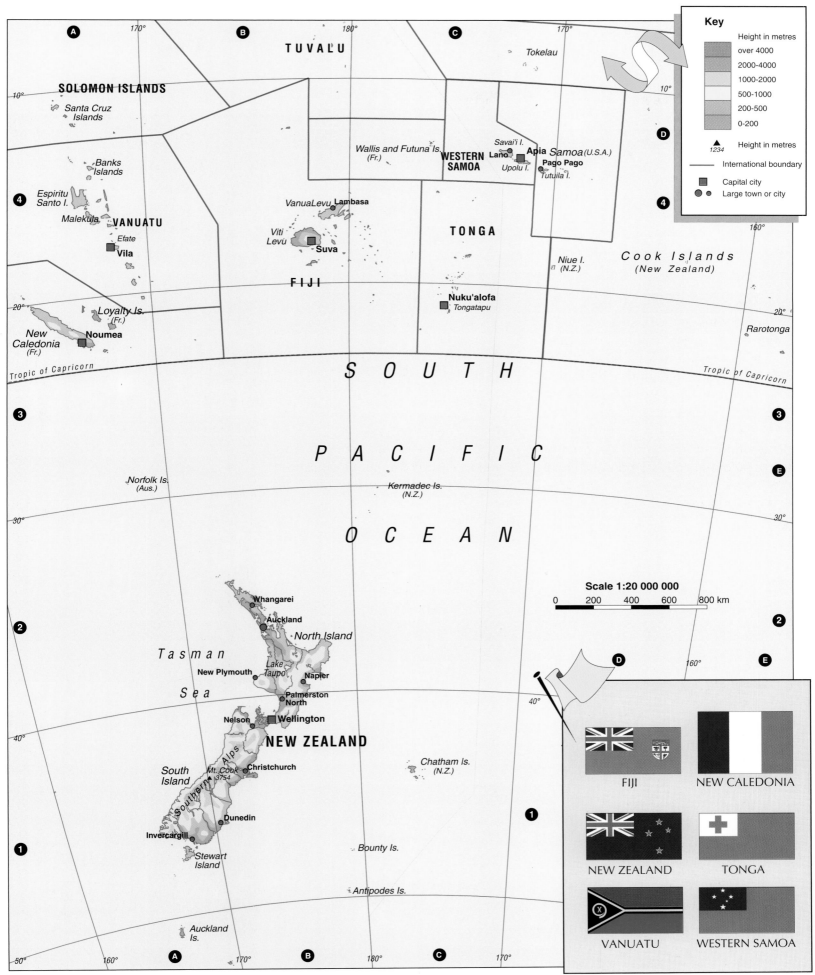

Key

Height in metres
- over 4000
- 2000-4000
- 1000-2000
- 500-1000
- 200-500
- 0-200

▲ Height in metres
1234

International boundary

■ Capital city

● ● Large town or city

TUVALU

SOLOMON ISLANDS

Santa Cruz Islands

Tokelau

Banks Islands

Wallis and Futuna Is. (Fr.)

WESTERN SAMOA

Savai'i I.
Lano
Apia Samoa (U.S.A.)
Upolu I.
Pago Pago
Tutuila I.

Espiritu Santo I.

VANUATU

Malekula

Efate
■ Vila

VanuaLevu Lambasa

Viti Levu

■ Suva

TONGA

Niue I. (N.Z.)

Cook Islands (New Zealand)

FIJI

Loyalty Is. (Fr.)

New Caledonia (Fr.)

■ Noumea

Nuku'alofa
Tongatapu

Rarotonga

Tropic of Capricorn

SOUTH

Tropic of Capricorn

PACIFIC

Norfolk Is. (Aus.)

Kermadec Is. (N.Z.)

OCEAN

Scale 1:20 000 000

0   200   400   600   800 km

Whangarei

Auckland

North Island

Tasman

New Plymouth
Lake Taupo
Napier

Sea

Palmerston North

Nelson
■ Wellington

NEW ZEALAND

Chatham Is. (N.Z.)

South Island

Mt. Cook 3754

Christchurch

Southern Alps

Dunedin

Invercargill

Bounty Is.

Stewart Island

Antipodes Is.

Auckland Is.

FIJI   NEW CALEDONIA

NEW ZEALAND   TONGA

VANUATU   WESTERN SAMOA

Antarctica

Antarctica is the continent surrounding the South Pole. In land area it is bigger than Europe. Antarctica is covered by a huge sheet of ice which is over 4500 metres thick in some places. In the winter months the ice sheet grows in size till it spreads nearly 1000 kilometres into the sea. Nearly all the world's ice is found in Antarctica.

The lowest ever temperature was recorded at Vostok base in 1988 at minus 89 degrees centigrade. In the winter there are four months when the sun never rises above the horizon and it is continually dark. Antarctica is the coldest, windiest place on earth. The only plants are mosses and lichens, but around the coasts there are great numbers of sea birds, seals, penguins and fish. The only people who live in Antarctica are the scientists who study the wild-life, rocks and weather. Because of the weather the scientists have to live in special buildings.

Antarctica is the last great wilderness on earth, but it is also very rich in mineral resources. There is a coalfield under the Transantarctic Mountains, copper and iron in the land around the Weddell Sea and oilfield under the sea near the coast.

There are no countries in Antarctica but because of the rich mineral resources many countries have laid claims to different parts of the continent. Since 1961 Antarctica has been governed by a special treaty in which countries have agreed that it should be set aside for peaceful purposes such as scientific research. At a conference in 1991 it was agreed that mining in Antarctica would be banned for the next 50 years. This is an important step in protecting the environment. Because of the low temperatures and dry, cold winds the environment is very fragile. It can take ten years for a footprint made in the moss to disappear.

Most birds on Antarctica are penguins. The main types are Adelie, Chinstrap, Emperor, Gentoos, King, Macaroni and Rockhopper. The photograph shows Adelie penguins going to their resting grounds.

Tourist planes and ships frequently visit Antarctica, particularly to the Antarctica Peninsula which has a slightly milder climate than the rest of Antarctica.

This photo shows the marker for the South Pole surrounded by the flags of some of the many countries that have laid claim to parts of Antarctica.

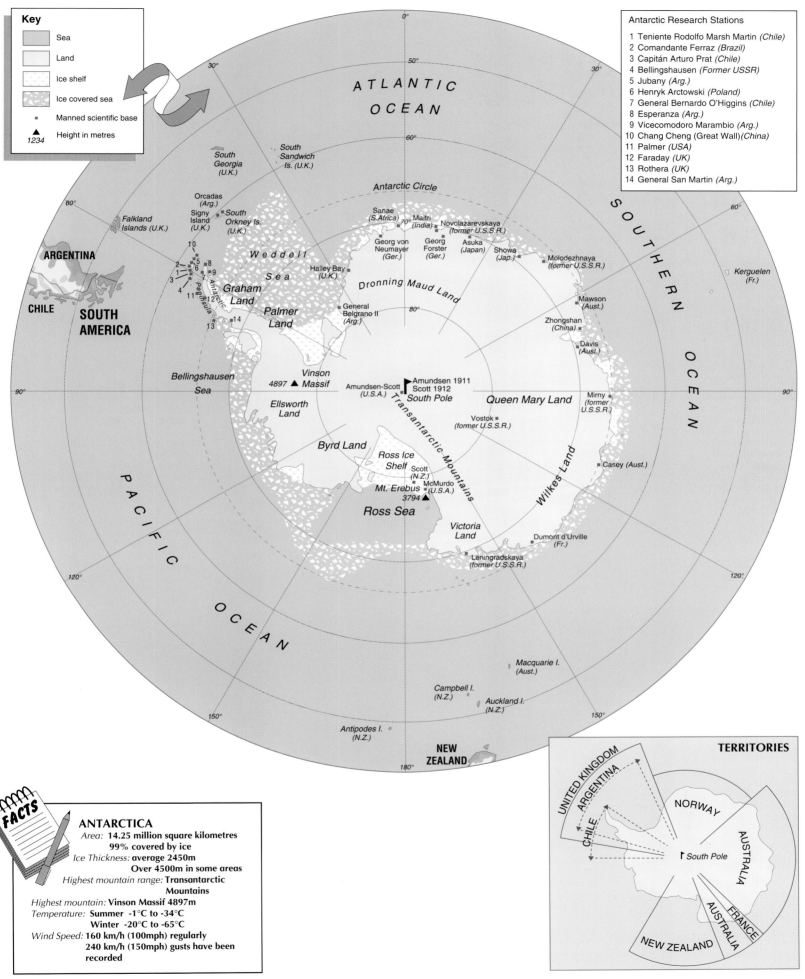

Key

- Sea
- Land
- Ice shelf
- Ice covered sea
- ■ Manned scientific base
- ▲ Height in metres
- *1234*

Antarctic Research Stations

1 Teniente Rodolfo Marsh Martin *(Chile)*
2 Comandante Ferraz *(Brazil)*
3 Capitán Arturo Prat *(Chile)*
4 Bellingshausen *(Former USSR)*
5 Jubany *(Arg.)*
6 Henryk Arctowski *(Poland)*
7 General Bernardo O'Higgins *(Chile)*
8 Esperanza *(Arg.)*
9 Vicecomodoro Marambio *(Arg.)*
10 Chang Cheng (Great Wall) *(China)*
11 Palmer *(USA)*
12 Faraday *(UK)*
13 Rothera *(UK)*
14 General San Martin *(Arg.)*

ATLANTIC OCEAN

0°
30°
50°
60°

Antarctic Circle

South Georgia (U.K.)
South Sandwich Is. (U.K.)

Orcadas (Arg.)
Signy Island (U.K.)
South Orkney Is. (U.K.)

Falkland Islands (U.K.)

ARGENTINA

CHILE

SOUTH AMERICA

SOUTHERN OCEAN

Kerguelen (Fr.)

Sanae (S.Africa)
Maitri (India)
Novolazarevskaya (former U.S.S.R.)
Georg von Neumayer (Ger.)
Georg Forster (Ger.)
Asuka (Japan)
Showa (Jap.)
Molodezhnaya (former U.S.S.R.)

Weddell Sea

Graham Land

Palmer Land

Dronning Maud Land

Halley Bay (U.K.)

General Belgrano II (Arg.)

Antarctic Peninsula

Mawson (Aust.)

Zhongshan (China)

Davis (Aust.)

Vinson 4897 ▲ Massif

Amundsen-Scott (U.S.A.)

Amundsen 1911
Scott 1912
South Pole

Queen Mary Land

Mirny (former U.S.S.R.)

Bellingshausen Sea

Ellsworth Land

Transantarctic Mountains

Vostok (former U.S.S.R.)

90°

Byrd Land

Ross Ice Shelf

Scott (N.Z.)

Mt. Erebus 3794 ▲

McMurdo (U.S.A.)

Casey (Aust.)

Wilkes Land

PACIFIC OCEAN

Ross Sea

Victoria Land

Dumont d'Urville (Fr.)

Leningradskaya (former U.S.S.R.)

120°
150°
180°

Macquarie I. (Aust.)

Campbell I. (N.Z.)

Auckland I. (N.Z.)

Antipodes I. (N.Z.)

NEW ZEALAND

FACTS

ANTARCTICA

Area: **14.25 million square kilometres**
99% covered by ice
Ice Thickness: **average 2450m**
Over 4500m in some areas
Highest mountain range: **Transantarctic Mountains**
Highest mountain: **Vinson Massif 4897m**
Temperature: **Summer -1°C to -34°C**
Winter -20°C to -65°C
Wind Speed: **160 km/h (100mph) regularly**
240 km/h (150mph) gusts have been recorded

TERRITORIES

UNITED KINGDOM
ARGENTINA
CHILE
NORWAY
AUSTRALIA
FRANCE
AUSTRALIA
NEW ZEALAND

South Pole

Index

Index

Test your Geographical Knowledge

QUESTIONS

51 Name the capital of North Korea.

52 Name two languages spoken in the Republic of Ireland.

53 Which European country has over 60,000 lakes?

54 What were the names given to London and Paris by the Romans?

55 In which two countries does the Aral Sea lie?

56 What island is known as the 'Pearl of the Indian Ocean'?

57 In what year will Hong Kong become part of China again?

58 Where is Burundi?

59 What does apartheid mean?

60 Which country has a capital called Asuncion?

61 Who were the first Europeans to reach Australia?

62 In which country is the headquarters of the Red Cross?

63 Which two countries are on the Iberian Peninsula?

64 In which African country was the world's largest deposit of manganese found?

65 Into what Gulf does the River Mississippi flow?

66 Where is St. Kitts-Nevis?

67 Name the largest lake in North America.

68 How many continents are there?

69 From what is coral made?

70 What currency is used in Latvia?

71 What are the three groups of people in Bosnia-Herzegovina?

72 In India what begins in June and lasts four months?

73 Which country uses the currency called Metical?

74 Which Pacific islanders were excellent navigators?

75 Name an Australian gold town.

76 Name the mountain range in north east Spain.

77 What does the DC of Washington DC stand for?

78 What is the name of the river that flows through Belorussia and Ukraine into the Black Sea?

79 What are the two names for the main islands that make up New Zealand?

80 In which century did France become a republic?

81 Which mountains separate Europe and Asia?

82 What country has a rising sun on its flag?

83 Which is the highest active Volcano in the world?

84 How many species of flowering plants are found in Brazil?

85 What is the worlds largest island?

86 Which small country lies between Austria and Switzerland?

87 Which three countries are sometimes called the 'Low Countries'?